Voice Tantra, Yoga Mantra
(Harmony of Inner and Expressed Voice)

By

Dr. Manjiree Vikas Gokhale
Ph.D (Music)

A book on Effective Techniques of Yoga for Voice, Communication, Expression and Creativity

Published by

Centre for Music and Healing

Saunvad – Centre for Music and Healing
Let your body and soul be in harmony

Copyright   :   Dr. Manjiree Vikas Gokhale
                         12, Anupam Society, Panchpakhadi,
                         Thane – 400602, India
                         Tel: 91-22-25432188 / Mobile: 91-9987764609
                         Website : www.manjireegokhale.com
                         Email   : manjireegokhale@yahoo.com

Published by   :   Dr. Manjiree Vikas Gokhale,
                         Saunvad Centre for Music and Healing, Thane

Printed from   :   Maharashtra Printers & Advertisers, Thane
                         Phone No. :- 9122-25408299

Cover Design   :   Roots Designs Studio, Thane
                         Mobile No.: 9619404433

First Published   :   28 March 2011

Editor   :   Roots Designs Studio, Thane

ISBN Number   :   978-93-81205-14-3

Price   :   ₹ 200/-

Available from   :   Author, www.amazon.com
                         www.Power-Publishers.com
                         www.flipkart.com

Supportive Audio & Video available with the author:
Audio cd   :   Guided Meditation on sound and
                         Guided Yoganidra (relaxation technique)
Video dvd   :   Demonstrations of Yoga Techniques and
                         general Voice Exercises

आता अभिनव वाग्विलासिनी जे चातुर्यार्थ
कलाकामिनी
ते श्री शारदा विश्वमोहिनी नमिली मियां ||

aataa abhinava vaagvilaasinI, je chaturyartha kalaa kaaminI,
te shrI shaaradaa vishwamihinI, namilI miyan ।।

(Marathi shloka-s from Jnaneshwari by Sant Jnaneshwar)

**Meaning: Now I bow to Godess Sharada, who
plays with the speech and desires the four arts
and who has mesmerized the whole
world with them.**

महर्षी पतंजली

योगेन चित्तस्य पदेन वाचां मलंशरीरस्य च वैद्यकेन ।
योऽपाकरोत्तं प्रवरं मुनीनां पतंजली
प्रांजलीरानतोऽस्मि ॥

yogenachittasya padenavacham malam sharIrasya cha vaidyakena
yopaakarottam pravaram munInaam patanjalI pranjalI raanatosmi

Meaning: I earnestly bow to Patanjali Muni who has given Yoga for the cleansing of Chitta, Grammer for the cleansing of Voice (speech) and medical science (Ayurveda) to remove the toxins of the body.

Dedicated to my Father-in Law

Late Bhau Gokhale

Alias

Shri Vinayak Ganesh Gokhale

I seek his blessings

Author's Profile

Dr. Manjiree Gokhale

- Done Ph.D. in Music from SNDT University, Mumbai. Topic - Importance of Yoga to Singers, with special refrence to Voice Culture. Completed M.A. in Hindustan Classical Vocals from the same university.
- Voice Trainer and Yoga Therapist – Specializing in Yoga for voice, speech, singing, hearing, enhancing musical perception, expression, communication, creativity, any voice problems (speaking or singing), voice modulation, articulation, phonation, improving breathing capacity, breath control, etc.
- Helps in healing Stammering, Thyroid and Asthma Patients also
- Music Teacher - Hindustan Classical, Popular Music (Hindi & Marathi)
- Teaching Devotional Music since 15 years
- Performer - Singer: Light and Devotional. Music
- Has performed/taught at several places in Maharashtra and outside including Kolhapur, Ratnagiri, Nagpur, Pandharpur, Goa and Chennai. Our Bhajan group has also performed on television channels.
- Healer and Counselor
- Gives personal guidance and/or training Past Life Regression Therapist and Trainer: Personal and Group Healing Sessions, lectures for awareness of past life regression as a therapy and clearing the misconceptions about it. Trained by Dr. Newton Kondaveti.
- Breathwork Rebirther - Healing through breathing techniques
- Reiki Master and Teacher.
- Research in Music Therapy, Medical Astrology and Past Life Regression Healing.
- Conduct workshops (both non-residential and residential)and Courses on Yoga for Voice Culture.

I love to conduct workshops, on musical subjects many,
Based on performance and theory, you can choose any.

Subjects like devotional music, and light to classical singing,
Music therapy, yoga 'n omkar, Voice culture are my liking

Be you new or experienced, In the field of music or not,
Training of 'Yoga' indeed, will make you different a lot.

Yoga has the ability, its one of the sure shot ways
To take you to musical depths, an experience you'll cherish always.

Contents

Author's Note

Purpose of the book
Swami Anubhavananda has said in his lectures on 'Yoga Research and Value Education', that in real Yoga Research, the 'Self' should be our laboratory and field of work. The research methodologies should be proved on 'Self'. The research should prove to balance ourselves more and more and to help us to improve our problems skillfully day by day.

'Yoga' is a perfect balance. Though later evolved especially for spiritual enlightenment, we should remember that 'yoga' since Vedic times was taught as an art of living. It has solutions for all colours of life and covers all aspects of our living styles. Voice and Music, are no exception.

Since childhood, I have been following the Yoga research methodology Swami Anubhavananda has mentioned. I have experienced the 'proof' in this 'Self' laboratory, which has led to my Voice Culturing and this book.

'Voice Tantra, Yoga Mantra' is a revised and edited version of my Ph.D. research thesis, 'Importance of Yoga to Singers, with special reference to Voice Culture'.

Beginning of the research:
I have trusted the therapeutic value of Yoga since I was a child. Being a person with 'Self Esteem', I have always liked to solve my problems on my own, using the 'Trial and Error' method with the help of ancient Ayurvedic, musical, Yogic and other spiritual scriptures.

My Ph.D. research thesis, 'Importance of Yoga to Singers, with special reference to Voice Culture', was like an elaborate report of my long research, done initially on myself. The same was later extended for experimental basis and on a larger scale, to the society, during my Ph.D. tenure. The story behind this research will surely prove beneficial to one and all.

To trace down the roots, I need to start with the problems I faced since I was a child. I am of course only quoting the problems related to 'Voice', and my speaking and singing abilities.

Problems Faced:
As a music student, learning vocal music (classical and light), I faced many difficulties like very bad breathing capacity, very bad audio memory, a bad memory in general, very small vocal range, harsh and extra base voice, lacking energy in my voice, difficulty in singing tana-s (quick notes), murki-s and khatka-s (special type of musical jerks), difficulty in picking up 'tala' (a complex rhythm pattern, though I was very good at 'laya' i.e. tempo), very weak physical strength including strength of the larynx, etc. Similarly, in my daily work schedule, I lacked the power of expression and communication in speaking as well as writing. I was rarely able to express or communicate, speak or write my thoughts exactly as I wanted to. The pinch that 'I did not mean this' or the thought 'it is on the tip of my tongue, but...' always remained my problem. I followed the traditional rectification exercises taught by my music teachers to overcome my problems. I also studied contemporary voice culture techniques and practiced many speech and vocal exercises. For expression and communication I tried out speech development programmes. But in spite of trying very hard and doing daily practice, the problems remained as they were. In fact, the more I tried, the problems seemed to worsen. Eventually, I had totally lost my voice and ability to speak and sing. I was quite depressed and went to an ENT surgeon. Unfortunately, even after a year long treatment, he was unable to solve any of my problems.

This triggered my self esteem. With total determination, I stopped all these treatments. I was a keen yoga follower and decided to solve my problems with the help of yoga. With this hypothesis, that yoga being holistic should help remove any discomfort and solve any problem including my voice, speaking and singing problems, **the foundation for my research was laid unintentionally.**

My studies followed a holistic pattern mentioned here. I would try to sing phrases which were either hard or not possible. One after another, I would sing each phrase, trying to search within, the root cause of the problem, with the help of inner awareness. Having derived a conclusion, I would then study and search for yogic practices suitable to remove that particular problem and then practice them for a week. After this practice, I would again try and sing that particular difficult piece of music, and with inner awareness, try to see if there was any positive difference happening. If the answer would be 'no' then repeat the process till I get positive results. This was my research methodology, the 'Trial and Error' method.

Fruits of Research:
I found that, that which I could not achieve with immense and long practices was achieved within a very short span of time with the help of yoga.

These positive changes provoked me to do a deeper and deeper research. I thought of giving these research experiences an experimental touch and penning it down systematically, So that more people should benefit from this research. This led me to my Ph.D. on this particular subject.

I was able to complete the research thesis, with the help of my yoga and music teachers.

Limitations:
I am fully aware that this book is not exhaustive for Voice Culture. Research, learning and growing is an endless process. As every person and every problem is unique, the answer, i.e. the 'yoga practice' design, to a particular problem for different persons should be unique and designed differently. There can

never be standardizations in yoga. I would be happy to see people doing more and more yoga and research with different aspects of yoga and making 'yoga' a part of each and every vocal activity.

I have designed listening tests for understanding our hearing ability. I have used them successfully in my research.

I believe that research is an ongoing process, as the world is ever changing. The principles behind the change, the laws of nature remain constant.

Expected Reader and Beneficiaries
This book is meant for people who want to develop their voice, expression, communication and creativity. It is also meant for people who would like to understand and learn new concepts of Yoga and Voice.

Contemporary Speech Therapists, Ear Trainers, ENT Surgeons, Physicians, Medical Practitioners, Yoga Therapists, Holistic Healers, etc. can read and understand these techniquies. They are welcome to integrate this knowledge in their daily healing or medical practice.

People working in the field of Voice like Singers, Actors, Teachers, Professors, Advocates, Sales and Marketing Personals, Orators, Politicians, etc. all can benefit by following the Yoga techniques mentioned in this book.

All other communities like students, house makers (housewifes), senior citizens, people with voice disorders of any type, thyroid patients, astham patients, etc. will benefit by these techniques.

This book is totally experience based. I am not trying to 'prove' any concepts, nor am I vouching these techniques. It is an action taken for sharing my experiences and understanding.

Sanskrit Script and Transliteration
In the first two Chapters Sanskrit words are given in italics. In the following Chapters though, the words are written normally.

The spellings used for these words are the spellings commonly used by the modern internet users, which is phonetic based. All proper nouns and 'concept' words start with a capital. Only the Shloka-s have been systematically transliterated by traditional method.

Sharing:
'Sharing' is one of the greatest virtues. I would be very happy to share this research with as many people as possible. It would be my pleasure to see people improving their voice qualities, as well as their emotional and behavioral qualities, by making yoga a part of their daily routine including music practice.

Let your body and soul be in harmony.

Love to one and all.

Dr. Manjiree Vikas Gokhale
Ph.D. (Music)
March 2011

Residential Address:
12, Anupam Society, Panchpakhadi,
Thane 400602
India
Phone: 91-22-25432188

Acknowledgements

It is my great pleasure to express my gratitude to all those who have helped me in publishing this book. This book is a collective effort of many people.

I would like to express my gratitude to my father, Swami Anand Rishi and mother, Sheelavati Khare, who are my inspiration to this book and my experimentation and research of yoga.

I invoke and thank the Spiritual Masters, specially Osho, Krishna, Saibaba of Shirdi and Reiki Master Dr. Mikao Usui, for guiding me in healing my own Voice, connecting my Vaikhari with my Inner Voice and subsequently 'Spiritual Search' throughout the path of this research and this book. In fact, I am just a messenger of all the material in this book. All these ideas and inspiration, is but their blessing.

I thank all my teachers, including my Yoga, Healing and Music teachers and all those who have helped me in some way or the other to complete this book and my research.

I am grateful to Dr. Neera Grover, my Ph.D. guide. Without her guidance and support it would not have been possible to complete my Ph.D. I am very much obliged to her.

I am very much thankful to all my family members for helping me directly or indirectly. I thank my husband, Vikas Gokhale for giving me moral support and backing during every difficulty in culturing the voice and speech. I thank my daughter, Ruta Gokhale and my daughter-in-law, Ruhi Gokhale for helping me in the process of publishing this book. I thank my son, Rishabh Gokhale, especially for giving me technical support.

I also thank my friends Deepali Manjrekar, Dr. Anuradha Gawade for their valuable advice and Upendra Gore for helping me in the DTP work and cover design.

I would like to thank the team of Maharashtra Printers & Advertisers who have helped me in publishing and printing this book.

Last but not the least I thank my sisters, mother-in-law and all my friends and relatives for supporting me where ever needed, bearing with my non-participation in many family and social functions, caused by the time restraint due to my busy schedules. They have been very understanding with me.

Let your body and soul be in harmony.

I thank one and all once again.

Dr. Manjiree Vikas Gokhale
Ph.D. (Music)
March 2011

Illustrations

Charts

Chapter I
The Voice – Its Importance

A. Voice as a Musical Instrument

Voice is a blessing to the mankind. No other living being is blessed with such quality. Voice is the medium of communication, the power of expression. The voice connects the head with the heart. It lies between them. It connects the intellect with emotions. It expresses the understanding and thoughts of the head with words. It connects our inner self with the outer world. It is a bridge between them. A developed voice means better expression and communication skills. A good voice leads to better expression. A flexible voice makes us capable of communicating in any given circumstance. A good voice helps us to master any situation by our expression skills.

Though basically used for speaking, voice is also used artistically for singing, i.e. to produce music. When the phonation is in a definite frequency, or a series of musical, sweet sounds, it is termed as singing.

The origin of Indian music lies in chanting of the mantras of *Sama Veda*.

The process of enriching the voice is known as voice culture. It involves training the voice to speak or sing in a particular desired way. It is a procedure where one learns to master one's voice. This study includes traditional and scientific methods to improve the quality of voice.

B. Voice - Speaking and Singing

The primary aim of 'voice' is communication and expression. But, the subtler qualities of voice are creativity, understanding of depth and details of sound and music. Improving speech and singing ability is a step towards this creative understanding.

Our speaking and singing voices are created from the same, exact anatomical structures. The respiratory system – lungs, diaphragm and abdominal muscles, the laryngeal mechanism – vocal folds, laryngeal cartilages, muscles and nerves and the supraglottic tract (the spaces above the vocal cords), including the back of our throat, mouth, tongue, teeth, nasal passages and sinus cavities, all work together to produce our beautiful voice.

Speaking does not require as much lung pressure as singing needs. In particular, classical singing needs still more lung pressure than folk or light style of singing. The speaking voice needs extra support of articulators for better articulation and phonation skills. Singing involves the utilization of more of the supraglottic spaces for resonance and the vowels are prolonged systematically. Otherwise, singing and speaking are almost identical.

We can find our natural pitch range for speaking by listening to how we spontaneously say the sound "hmm-mm", when we are in a jovial and happy mood. The top note of our "hmm" is a good place to start. We should try to sustain the pitch of the "hmm" and move into a phrase we would typically say. For example, "hmm-mm - how are you?" If this pitch range differs substantially from the pitch we typically use when speaking, we are not at an optimal pitch and could be straining our voice to maintain that pitch. Other indicators of natural pitch can be our laugh or cough. Though these are not scientifically proven systems of finding our correct pitch, they are very much reliable. Our habitual pitch may or may not be our optimal i.e. natural pitch.

Just a note: Ideally, our speaking and singing voice should sound almost identical in pitch.

C. Voice and its Extended Meaning

'Voice' in a larger sense, extends its scope and is responsible for expression, communication and abstract creativity. The holistic meaning of Voice is the creative expression and communication through either voice or any abstract skills. We can improve upon all these skills. These qualities are not interdependent. They are different aspects of Voice. Improving upon any of these is always supportive for all Voice related activities. This also facilitates the working of these skills.

In this larger sense, all our motor organs and our hands and all the body movements and gestures are also an extension of expression, communication and creativity. From this point onwards, in this book the word 'voice' would always be used in its larger sense, expect in the topics related to contemporary anatomy and physiology.

D. Importance of Voice for All

The importance of developing speaking voice for an actor and singing voice for a singer can be easily understood. But, it becomes important to understand that developing the speaking voice for everyone including a singer and developing singing voice for everyone including an actor is equally essential. This is because good speaking voice makes each ones' expression and communication more effective. Similarly, developing musical voice and skills help us in harmonizing our body and mind.

Hence, Voice should be trained and cultured for better communication, speaking and singing skills. Effective control of breath, enhancing breathing capacity and sound perception, flexible speech organs, adjustments of resonators, wider voice range, mental perception, etc. are the common features wherein the voice can be trained.

Though voice is used for both speaking and singing, the

The Voice - Its Importance

technique of voice production for singing is more complex. Singing requires a more delicate control over the muscles and a more complex pattern of their coordination with the brain.

Voice production consists of many fields for training such as the shape of the mouth, effective pronunciation of the words, adjusting the voice to different tempos or speeds, controlling of volume or amplitude as the background of presentation demands, good pronunciation, a very important feature of developing imaginative power to improvise, and above all a better analytical hearing capacity of all the above factors.

The voice has to be trained according to the style and type of expression one chooses, e.g. speaking, singing, oration, narration, drama, etc. This is because each type of expression demands a different style of voice production. Hence, the training style will also differ.

Every individual is unique, so is every voice. Though there are individual limitations differing from person to person, it is very important to note that Voice can be cultivated, improved and cultured, by variation of pitch, intensity and timbre (tonal quality) at any age.

E. Features of Voice-Training

1. Hearing:
Hearing is the initial step in training the Voice. The better we train our ears, better will be our voice production capacity.

Hearing is subdivided in four parts: Hearing, Listening, Perceiving and Storing.

i. Hearing: It is the physical process of receiving sound waves through the ears.
ii. Listening: It is a step further. Our mind decides as to which sounds should be attended to and which ones to be

filtered and ignored. Concentrated listening is an important requirement.

iii. Perceiving: The process of perceiving starts once this decision of filtration is taken. This is the process of analysis and interpretation of the filtered sound. The chosen sound is analyzed by the brain in as many ways as possible. The brain has emotional centres which are aroused by the sound. The analyzed sound is thus emotionally labeled. The analysis depends on all the knowledge gathered by the brain, both musical and non-musical. This analysis can be enhanced by proper training. Then, according to our likes, dislikes, emotions and preferences, the analyzed sound is interpreted. eg. The interpretation of the same, small, simple musical piece by a North Indian Classical Singer will differ from that of a Pop Singer.

iv. Storing: Storing is the completion stage of hearing. Once the perceiving happens, the sound is stored in the brain, in the form of vibratory patterns called as memory. These patterns are formed by a combination of senses. The ability of all the five senses depends upon 'learning', environment, upbringing, training, etc. These capacities can be enhanced and improved.

The sound is analyzed in as many ways as it is trained to do so. The storing may be in the form of audio or visual memory. Sound can also be perceived and stored by other senses. The notes, the tunes, the rhythm, the speed, the words, the volume, the tonal quality of the voice or instrument, etc. all are stored separately in the brain.

When we try to speak or sing, these mental images are memorized at will and coordinated with the respiratory and laryngeal muscles to produce required voice. Hence, the more we hear, the more we listen, and the better we perceive, there will be a better ability of voice production. We should listen by giving attention to all the aspects of voice and singing, like, tonal quality, phonetic quality, time intervals, the microtones (*shruti-s*), expressional effects of the voice, volume, pitch, etc. The more analytically we listen with utmost concentration and understanding better will be our sound perception, following a better quality of voice production. Similarly, better the mental and physical coordination better will be the voice production.

It is a well known fact that deaf people are also dumb. Most of the time, this dumbness is not because of a structural disorder, but, it is usually due to the inability to hear. This explains the importance of hearing in any voice activity. As stated above, the more we increase the quality of our hearing capacity, better will be the quality of voice production.

Though this is the first, basic, fundamental and unavoidable step towards learning, we should remember that this is not the only step. It is not enough by itself.

2. Breathing Capacity and Control of Breath:
Good breathing capacity along with good control of breath is very important for voice production. Our voice production directly depends on these capacities. Breathing affects the air pressure and air volume capacity necessary for voice production. Apart from this, good and proper breathing helps develop all the muscles necessary for breathing, as proper breathing is a natural exercise to the entire respiratory tract.

It is alarming and unbelievable to know that usually, in daily life patterns, proper breathing is not taught. Very few people naturally breathe properly and fully. Studies have also shown that we use as less as only 25% of our total breathing capacity. Total Breathing capacity is the Lung capacity (see Chapter 2 for details). It is the amount of air that the lungs (the air sacs) can contain at any given time. Most of the times, more than half of the air sacs stay unused. So the importance of learning to breathe properly is very important. When we say that there is an increase in the Breathing Capacity, it the Optimal

Breathing Capacity we increase. It is the normal breathing capacity plus the active capacity in the reserve volumes, used whenever needed during physical activities. It should not be mistaken as the Total Lung Capacity, which cannot be altered. During normal breathing we use the Tidal Volume. But, when we do physical activity we use the active air sacs in the reserve volumes, as much as the need arises. When we say that the Optimal Volume increases, it means increase of the Tidal Volume plus the capacity to use more and more of the unused Alveolar Air (or air sacs) during breathing.

Breathing can be divided in 4 types:
i.   Abdominal breathing
ii. Diaphragmatic breathing
iii. Costal or Chest breathing
iv. Clavicular or Shoulder breathing

There are many differences of opinions between scholars regarding the types of breathing and also their importance in voice production and culturing. Some therapists do not make a difference in Diaphragmatic and Abdominal breathing, though personally, I treat them differently. I have experienced with the help of inner awareness that both breathing types give different results.

Many scholars believe that Abdominal breathing, if practiced regularly and properly, is enough by itself as a holistic type of breathing. Personally, I disagree with this view. Not because I have some research based conclusions, but, because I have experienced myself that the other three types of breathing also, have improved my voice quality, confidence, ability to sing fast musical phrases and much more.

i. Abdominal breathing is **vertical** breathing, exerting pressure to the diaphragm and further to the abdominal muscles. It develops the strength and capacity of the abdominal muscles and the diaphragm. Like diaphragmatic breathing it activates the lower part of the lungs. As the movements of the diaphragm are dependent on the strength of the abdominal muscles this type of breathing is very important for all vocal activities, for good voice production. This type of breathing helps us to produce the lower notes effectively and helps improve our health in general. This also helps to develop a strong voice and helps in enhancing lower harmonics to the voice which give a quality of depth to it. This also helps in developing the slow tempo (*vilambita laya*)

ii. Diaphragmatic breathing is a combination of Abdominal and Costal breathing but, giving special attention to the diaphragm. It is both **horizontal and vertical** breathing together. The air pressure is distributed horizontally in the chest and vertically downwards, towards the diaphragm. It activates the air sacs in the lower part of the lungs. Along with intercostal muscles, it also makes the diaphragm strong and healthy, building up its muscular strength and muscle tone. This type of breathing is useful for each one of us. When we cultivate this type of breathing, unnecessary and unwanted wobbling or shaking of voice can be controlled. It gives a steadiness to the voice and consistency to its quality. This type of breathing is also useful to speak/sing quick words/notes in succession.

iii. Costal breathing or Chest breathing activates the air sacs and muscles of the middle part of the lungs. It is called as **horizontal** breathing, as the air pressure moves horizontally in the chest. It makes the intercostal muscles strong and healthy. This type of breathing is useful to produce high and middle pitched voice. It is also useful to give a strong voice which has optimum volume and also to have control over the volume, i.e. intensity.

iv. Clavicular breathing or Shoulder breathing activates the air sacs and muscles in the upper part of the lungs, near the shoulders. These air sacs need to be activated and are useful for producing very shrill and/or high-pitched voice. This breathing is also useful where the speaking or singing pattern does not allow enough time to breathe deeply, either because of negligible time interval between words or because of the very fast tempo of delivering notes and words, not allowing enough time-gap between words to breathe deeply.

Along with good breathing capacity we also need a **good control over the breath.** We need to gain mastery over the breathing in-and-out patterns. It is necessary to develop the skill of using a given amount of breath for a particular music or speech piece, in the best possible way. This needs a control over the chest muscles and the diaphragm. It is also necessary to have a skillful control of the time regulations of the air volume and pressure of breathing in and breathing out patterns. If we can master these breathing skills, we can easily master our voice. Breath Control gives fine-ness, clarity, steadiness and confident phonation to the voice. It develops a good tonal quality.

Breathing Capacity and Breath Control skills are independent aspects. They are two aspects of breathing, both necessary, individually and together, for voice production.

3.Practice:
Everyone knows – 'Practice makes a man perfect'. The mechanism of our body needs daily exercises to keep it fit and moving. Like any other machine, our body also needs daily maintenance.

Practice should be divided in basically two types:
i. Trying that which we cannot speak/sing, but wish to speak/sing.
ii. Repeating that which we already know and bring it closer to perfection.

Further this can be divided into seven sub-types:
i. Allotting special time to speak/sing in all octaves – lower, middle and higher - to develop the pitch range

ii. Allotting special time for all the tempos, to develop the tempo range

iii. Allotting special time for developing and maintaining the timbre, including volume fluctuations along the pitches and tempos. In other words allot time to develop a smooth register shifting.

iv. Allotting special time for the speaking/singing styles.

v. Allotting special time for singing without rhythm accompaniment (for singers).

vi. Allotting special time to sing with accompaniment (for singers).

vii. Allotting special time to develop improvisation (especially, in classical singing, narration and oration).

By regular practice of singing and voice modulation, we give physical training to all the muscles and the voice-production system on the whole. This training will vary with the type of spoken words or the music chosen for singing. The aspects of the voice, phonation, articulation and pitch-control vary with the style of music or speech piece, so will the factors to be emphasized vary during practice.

The time period that should be given for practice will again vary with the time span of the expected performance. In classical types of music where improvisation is a part of the performance, it is necessary to devote more time, even two or three hours at a stretch, with two or more of such sessions during the day, for practice to cover all the aspects of the performance. On the other hand, light music singer can complete his necessary daily training sessions, in as short as half an hours' span. Similarly, this pattern will apply to speech performances of long and short duration.

One important factor during practice is that we should, along with speaking/singing, learn to hear our own speech/singing, critically. We should listen like a third party, trying to find both the good and bad points of our speech/singing. This will help us to grow faster. We can liberally make use of the modern electronic and digital techniques to do this. We should thus find out our own mistakes and limitations and work over them. This would rule out overconfidence, and develop an understanding of the critics view. We should always remember that perfection is a word found only in the dictionary, it is but an illusion. If we start thinking that our performance is perfect, then the growing, culturing and cultivating totally stops. At any given point of time, there is always ample scope to learn. Voice has no limits in either of its aspects. So, the learning procedure should never come to an end.

Practice develops the control over the vocal cords. Practice also develops confidence in us, which is conveyed through the voice.

4. Physical and Mental Fitness:

Voice production is an activity of coordination of physical and mental movements. It depends on the combination of our physical and mental health. Hence, both physical and mental fitness are necessary for good and effective voice. In view of the fact that our voice should be rich with harmonics, all the resonators i.e. the air cavities in our body should be clean and healthy, free of all toxins. This specially include the lung cavities, sinuses, pharynx and nasal cavities, which are directly related to voice production. These resonators should be free from coughs and colds, extra mucus and other infections, for a good voice quality.

We experience that overwhelming emotions affect our voice controlling capacity. Negative emotions also affect the tonal quality of our voice. Negative emotions are a hindrance to good voice production. Mental fitness leads to a better synchronization of the vocal activities.

Regular exercise, healthy and balanced diet and regular

meditation or any stress-releasing exercises are a necessity for our fitness. *Yogaasana-s, Pranaayam,* or any other Yogic Practice is the best type of balanced and holistic exercise that can be beneficial to us.

5. Other Features Necessary for Voice Training

These features mainly depend upon the main features explained above. They are apparently included in those four main features. Also, some features are interdependent.

i. Musical Ear: It is the quality to be able to differentiate the changes in the pitch, volume, tempo and timbre of any sound and musical piece.

ii. Flexible Speech-organs: The speech organs include the phonation organs (vocal cords and larynx) and the articulators. Their flexibility decides the voice quality and phonation abilities.

iii. Resonators: The sinuses should be clear and should have soft walls. The adjustable resonators also should have soft and healthy walls and should be flexible to adjust to good quality resonation.

iv. Audio Memorization: All that is heard and perceived by the ear is stored in the brain. Whenever we wish to speak/sing, the brain reads the stored material and sends impulses to imitate the sound. This memory can be enhanced by developing all the five sensory input capacities of the sense organs. In Audio Memorization, memory can be Auditory, Visual, Emotional, Language or any type of Memory. We remember sound by associating it to any of these senses.

v. Good Posture: The lungs should be in their optimum capacity position. The larynx and chest should not be either compressed or stretched. The backbone must be erect. The body and mind should be relaxed and stress free.

vi. Smooth register shifting: While shifting from higher to lower pitch/notes or vice versa there should be a shift of registers. This shift should be such that it should not affect the tonal quality of the voice. It should be smooth, not jerky.

vii. Speech/Musical Ability: The ability is a combination of abilities to listen, perceive, interpret and reproduce words/music with details.

viii.   Creativity: It is the ability to create new permutations and combinations of words and music, as well as applying other knowledge and information creatively and artistically to speech or singing.

ix. Expression: It is the ability to express emotions while speaking or singing. It also includes the ability to express the image of expression created in the mind before actual expression.

x. Voice range: It is the range of notes a speaker/singer can speak/sing. A better range is the ability to speak/sing more and more notes of the upper and lower octaves clearly. The range of the voice can be altered and stretched by regular practice.

xi. Vocal/Musical Perception and Expression: It is dependant not only on the vocal/musical aspects of the learner but also many other aspects like environment, family background, economical status, social background, cultural background, etc.

F. Learning,   Teaching,   Writing/Composing   and Performing

Learning, Teaching, Writing (as an art/skill)/Composing and Performing are all aspects of speech/singing. They are not directly interdependent. They are independent in their basic nature. From all the four factors any one or a combination of any two, three or all the four may be present in a person. A person who is a good learner may or may not be a good performer or teacher or composer. Similarly, a good performer may or may not be a good learner, teacher or composer. This applies to a teacher and performer too. This happens because, it is practically very difficult for a person to observe and pay due importance and give required time to all the features mentioned in Voice Training. The parts of the brain and other physical activities required for the culturing of each of these abilities differ. Nevertheless, we can develop all these aspects together also. Though all the culturing aspects are important, the following aspects should be given more importance in the development of learning, teaching, writing/composing and performing

i. Learning: In learning all the five senses are involved. All the three aspects of hearing, practice and good posture are equally important to be a good learner. Open mindedness, which is a part of good mental health, is also important for learning to speak or sing. We need to develop the capacities of all our five senses. These senses are the passage for learning.

ii. Teaching: To develop good teaching skills we need to develop good memory, daily practice, patience, mental stability, fitness of larynx, expressional skills and some amount of creative thinking. A good teacher should be good at understanding and solving the difficulties of the student.

iii. Writing/Composing: Creativity is the most important factor to be emphasized and developed for good writing/composing. Hearing ample music and speech with its variations, and developing expressional skills is equally important.

iv. Performing: All aspects except Creativity are important. Creativity can be an additional qualification for excellence. Other skills like stage understanding and administrative skills are also necessary for becoming a successful performer. Having self esteem and confidence are other factors, a performer should never overlook.

G. Understanding, Reading and Writing Language or Music

Different parts of the brain are involved in each of these activities. These aspects are also independent in their basic nature. A person may possess any one, or a combination of these skills together. Each skill needs different factors to be emphasized for its development.

Perception and interpretation depend not only on learning the performing skills, but also its philosophy, theory and technique as well as all the other knowledge and experience we gather throughout our life. Better holistic perception, leading to better interpretation, further leads to better understanding. All these aspects are equally important. Ancient scholars have emphasized this fact.

Sound is perceived by our brain by combination of our senses and emotions. It is stored in different parts of the brain in different forms (see fig. 2.15). Memorizing of any sound is supported by all our five senses and emotions together. Reading or writing language or music helps in faster understanding and memorizing, with better accuracy. This is because visual memory helps in this mechanism. Hence, reading and writing language/music are important. This fact is explained more elaborately in Chapter II.G.1.iii and chart 2.3

H. References of Voice According in Various Texts

It is believed, that good voice is necessary for good speaking and singing. But, 'good' is an abstract, subjective and relative term. Secondly, the 'goodness' differs according to the style of speech/music. Thirdly, the concept of 'Good' voice varies from time to time and place to place. The anatomical, personal, social and situational ideals vary a lot. Few references of quality of good voice are given below.

1. Natyashashtra:

The most ancient and authoritative Indian text which talks about good voice is 'Natyashaashtra' (around 200B.C.) by Bharata Muni, also called as 'Natyaveda'. Bharata Muni has stated following six qualities of good voice for singers and actors, which are applicable to all of us.

श्रावकोऽथ घनः स्निग्धो मधुरोह्यवधानवान् ॥
त्रिस्थानशोभीत्येवं तु षट्कांगस्य गुणाः स्मरताः ॥ ३२.३३.११ ॥

shraavako-tha ghanah snigdho madhuro hyavadhaanavaan
tristaanashobhItyevam tu shatkangasya guNaah smarataah
|| 32.33.11 ||

meaning: Voice which can be well heard (loud enough), well tuned and
richly textured, smooth and that which is not harsh, is sweet and
harmonious, a voice well tuned and a voice which is balanced in all the
three octaves and registers – remember these are the six limbs or qualities
of good voice.

An important factor to be understood is that a good voice is
assumed to have **'all'** these qualities together.

i. Shravaka – Loud enough voice, which can be well heard
by the audience, even at a long distance, when necessary, is
called as *shravaka*. (Till recent times, as there was no sound
projection technology this quality was a necessity. Today,
though its importance is not less, it can be managed by
technological advances.)

ii. Ghana – *Ghana* voice is a pleasing and tuned voice.
This voice has a rich texture (especially which has a 'bass'
effect).

iii. Snigdha – The voice which sounds smooth, soft and
sweet, that which is not harsh is *snigdha*.

iv. Madhura – A voice that is melodious and harmonious
is called as *madhura*.

v. Avadhanavan – A voice that is sweet and
harmonious, a voice which knows how to tune itself
perfectly is termed as *avadhanavan*.

vi. Tristhanashobhi – This voice is properly balanced in
all the octaves and registers. The texture of this voice has
consistency in all three registers.

2. Sangeet Ratnakar:

Sharangadeo in his text 'Sangeet Ratnakar' (13th century A.D.)

gives more than thirty qualities of the voice. He says that basically voice is of three types, which bear the qualities of *kapha*, *pitta* and *vata*. Further, he says, they can be combined into infinite qualities of *mishraka* (combination) out of which he has stated only thirty due to limitation of space.

i. Khahula – Derived from *kapha*, having qualities of *snigdha*, *madhura* and *komala* i.e. soft, sweet and tender. This type of voice in lower (*mandra*) and middle (*madhya*) octave is called as *adilla*.

ii. Narata – Derived from pitta, it has qualities of *ghana*, *gambhira* and *Leena* (*asphuta*) i.e. rich textured, having good bass effect and humble.

iii. Bombaka – Derived from *vata*, it has qualities of *nihssara*, *kathora*, *tara* i.e. dry, harsh and high-pitched.

iv. Mishraka – Is any combination of above three qualities.

3. Other Ancient Texts:

There are many other texts which talk about good voice and good song (*ganam*) which includes qualities of voice also. But all of them talk about same or similar qualities eg. Naradiya Shiksha, Paniniya Shiksha, Sangeeta Samayasara of Parshvadeva, Manasollasa of Raja Someshwar, etc.

It should be noted that in these texts, these qualities were mentioned for classical singers and that in those ancient days, there were no inventions of audio technology.

4. Changes and Fluctuations by Time and Style

The concepts of qualities of a good voice, change according to the style of speech/singing. It differs from place to place, from east to west, from theater to home, from classical to folk and from ancient to recent times. We shall now consider some most common differences:

i. Today's Indian Classical Music still demands all the

ancient qualities. The quality of loudness though, in today's world, has not remained a necessity for performers. This is because of the advent of microphones and loudspeakers. They do the work of amplifying the voice. Still, the quality of loudness definitely adds to the luster of the voice and is considered good.

ii. As today's artists use microphones, their voice needs to be cultured with an additional improvement in a tonal quality suitable for the microphones. The intensity of many harmonics and overtones in our voice is beyond our normal hearing range. Microphones amplify even such overtones and harmonics that are otherwise not audible to a normal ear. Hence, the voice should be made so richly textured and so clean that no harsh harmonics are heard even by the microphone. The microphone amplifies the blasts and hisses in the voice, while pronouncing harsh alphabets like 'bha', 'tha', and hissing alphabets like 'sa', etc which are otherwise, not audible to the human ear.

iii. Falsetto' and 'crooning' are admitted in light and folk singing, and in tribal and rural speech, usually all over the world.

iv. In western type of singing 'vibrato' and 'tremolo' are admired as a good quality. They are different from the 'trembling' or shaking or wobbling which is the effect of incorrect breathing and weakness of the larynx. They are deliberate actions and need a strong larynx, correct breathing, and correct posture. 'Vibrato' and 'tremolo' are now getting rooted in music of India. These qualities are used in singing and drama for showing fear, unsteadiness, old age, etc. Even in olden Indian dramas and Cinema nasal speech and singing was appreciated.

v. In some types of singing nasality and shrillness are appreciated and admired in Japan, China, Arabia, Russia, Germany, France, etc. Folk

vi. In most styles of speech and music, frequent changes in registers are not appreciated. But, in Austrian singing 'yodeling', a technique which requires frequent changes of registers, is appreciated and admired.

vii. A deep, heavy and base voice, having abdominal and chest resonance, is appreciated in Indian classical music. But, in Indian light music, especially film music, a voice which is shallow, light and which has more head and nasal resonance is more appreciated. Similarly heaviness and lightness of voice will need to be changed according to the subject of speech.

viii. In today's Bollywood industry, harsh and husky voice and sometimes even breathy voice is also accepted and is in good demand.

As far as the singer is in tune, to the scale and in rhythm and a speaker is to the point, effective, convincing and using proper words, we have to remember that we should not label any voice as correct or incorrect. Of course, the voice should be suitable to the chosen style of speaking/singing and accepted by audience. 'Physiologically good phonation and articulation' is many times not appreciated, considered improper, or does not even give the required effect of the speech or music.

Usually, it is thought that once we develop one type of voice it is not possible to speak or sing in another style. But this is more a block of the mind than the physical problem. We can shape, and culture and make our voice so flexible that it can be effectively changed, according to the chosen music style. It is neither impossible, nor difficult. It is just a knack. It needs a flexible mind, flexible thinking style and of course enough practice and understanding of the required style.

I. The Basic Characteristics of Voice

Any sound including our voice has four basic characteristics, whether it is a speaking or a singing voice. A voice can be cultured as speaking, and from speaking to singing voice by fine tuning these qualities. It is necessary to work on all these aspects of voice separately and simultaneously to make the voice better and better.

i. Pitch or *swara*: The voice is either musical or non-musical with reference to the pitch mechanism (described further). This depends on the hearing capacity and a will to have a musical intonation of the voice, the desire to have a beautiful voice. The basic or optimum pitch of a voice is dependant on the laryngeal structure. It cannot be altered. But, the pitch rage, register shifting and quality of pitch throughout the full vocal rage of the voice can be developed and cultured by *yogasadhanaa*.

ii. Tempo or *laya*: The flow of voice is in-built with different combinations of *laya* i.e. tempo. The tempo is in the style of pronouncing each syllable, a consonant and its vowel, pauses between words and sentences, etc. When all the tempos together are integrated and balanced, then the *laya* becomes musical. This imbalance can be improved through awareness and practice of yoga.

iii. Volume or intensity: Each person's voice has an optimum volume or loudness of expression. It is unique for each person. This is the value which depends on the physical structure of the breath apparatus and other parts of the body and the general muscular, physical and mental fitness of a person. Except for the skeletal physical shape, all the other factors can be developed with yoga.

iv. Timbre or texture: This is the quality of voice or sound which enables us to distinguish the difference between two voices or sounds. A voice when produced brings along with it a series of harmonics and overtones. These harmonics and overtones are usually feeble to hear. The intensity of the fundamental note is always more than them. The relative intensity of these harmonics and overtones present in each voice influences the timbre. This is influenced by the physical structure, muscular strength, muscular tone and general physical and mental health and energy level. Like intensity, except for the skeletal physical shape all other factors can be developed with yoga. Also, except for the fundamental frequency, the relative intensity of the harmonics and the overtones can be developed with yoga.

J: Role of Yoga in Singing and Voice Culturing

Our physical body has an equivalent at the quantum level. Quantum is defined as the basic unit of matter or energy. It is from 10,000,000 to 100,000,000 times smaller than the smallest atom. All quanta are made of vibrations, both - visible and invisible, measurable and immeasurable vibrations. Energy which is invisible when needed takes physical or material form.

Physical structures can be changed faster and more easily by working on the quantum levels. Thanks to modern research and technology. Now, it has become easy to believe such facts laid by ancient Indian texts as they are being proven by contemporary technology. These facts were not only known but, mastered by *Yogi-s*, *Ayurvedacharya-s* (doctors of *Ayurveda*) and ancient musicians thousands of years before modern discoveries. Yoga explains these facts in the language of twenty-eight principles, elements and *Kosha-s*, *Chakra-s*, *Nadi-s*, etc. *Yoga* further explains different practices to be followed to bring about the intended changes.

It is these subtle quantum levels that hold greatest energy potentials. Yoga can heal these quantum levels and many changes including voice changes can be brought about on the gross level also.

To change the printout of our voice, we should learn to rewrite the software of our mind and intellect. *Yoga* is the process and key to open this door.

Chapter II
Anatomy and Physiology of Voice

In this Chapter we will be discussing the anatomy and physiology of all the main organs of the human body related with the production of speech and singing. The anatomy of speech and singing is the same. The difference lies in the physiology. Singing needs far more complex coordination and functional abilities.

A. Speech

Speech is one of the most complex and delicate operation that the body undertakes. Eventually, speech, talk and comprehension all are controlled and coordinated by the brain. In the cerebral cortex there are areas called the speech centres where words are deciphered and signals and instructions are

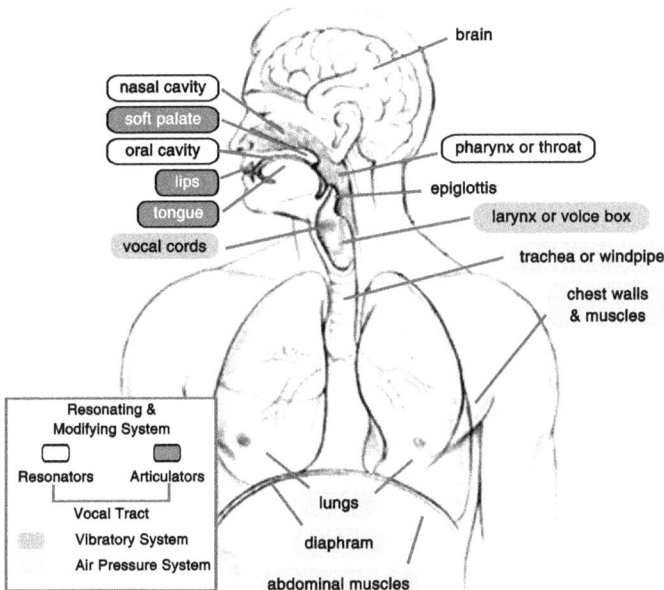

fig 2:1 - Voice Organs

Role of Voice Organs in Voice Production

System	Voice Organs	Role in Voice Production
Air pressure System	Diaphragm, Chest walls and muscles, ribs, abdominal muscles, Trachea, Lungs	Provides and regulates air pressure to cause vocal folds / cords to vibrate. Regulates 'Intensity'
Vibratory System	Voice box (larynx)	Vocal folds / cords vibrate, changing air pressure to sound waves producing "voiced sound," frequently described as a "buzzy sound" Regulates 'Pitch'
	Vocal cords	Regulates pitch of sound
Resonating System - Resonators	Vocal tract, throat (pharynx), oral cavity, nasal passages, sinuses, abdomen	Changes the "buzzy sound" into a person's recognizable voice. Regulate the 'timbre', texture of voice
Modifying System - Articulators	Oral Cavity (teeth, gums, cheeks, hard palate,), lips, tongue, soft palate, pharynx	Changes the phonated vowels to consonants. They modify the voiced sound. The articulators produce recognizable words. Regulate language
Sensory Input, Receiving System	Ears, all sense organs	Hearing, Listening, Perceiving
Master Organ	Brain,	Regulation and Coordination of all Sense and Motor Functions, Memory

chart 2:1

sent out to the hundreds of muscles in the lungs, throat and mouth that are involved in producing voice.

The whole of the respiratory system and the entire structure of the muscles from the abdomen to the brain play some part in the production of speech sounds. Fig. 2.1 and chart 2.1 explain the organs and their respective roles in the production of speech.

B. The Larynx

The larynx is positioned in the anterior neck, (see fig. 2.2) slightly below the point where the pharynx divides and gives rise to the separate respiratory and digestive tracts. Because of this location, the larynx plays a critical role in normal breathing, swallowing, and speaking. Damage to the larynx or its tissues can result in interference with any or all of these functions.

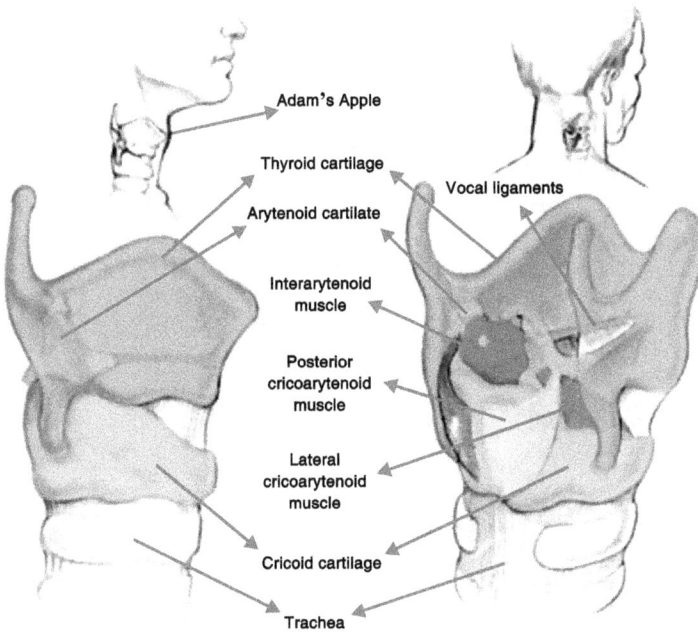

Adam's Apple

Thyroid cartilage

Vocal ligaments

Arytenoid cartilate

Interarytenoid muscle

Posterior cricoarytenoid muscle

Lateral cricoarytenoid muscle

Cricoid cartilage

Trachea

fig 2:2 larynx

The larynx is the body's voice box, containing the vocal cords, which vibrate to produce speech. As such, it is an extremely delicate instrument, but it also has another less complex function of guarding the entrance to the lungs by a valve called epiglottis.

When we eat or drink, the larynx closes tightly, making food or liquids slide over it, down into the esophagus (food pipe), which leads into the stomach. When we need to breathe in or out, of course it is open. The action of the epiglottis is automatically controlled by the brain, but sometimes it fails, and then liquids or food particles go down the 'wrong way'. Unless a lump of food is so large that it sticks in a passage below the larynx, it will be coughed back up.

The vocal cords lie in the centre of this framework in an anterior-posterior orientation. When viewed from above (see fig2.3) the right and left cords appear as a "V"-shaped structure, with the aperture between the "V" forming the entrance to the trachea. At the rear of the larynx on each side, each vocal cord is

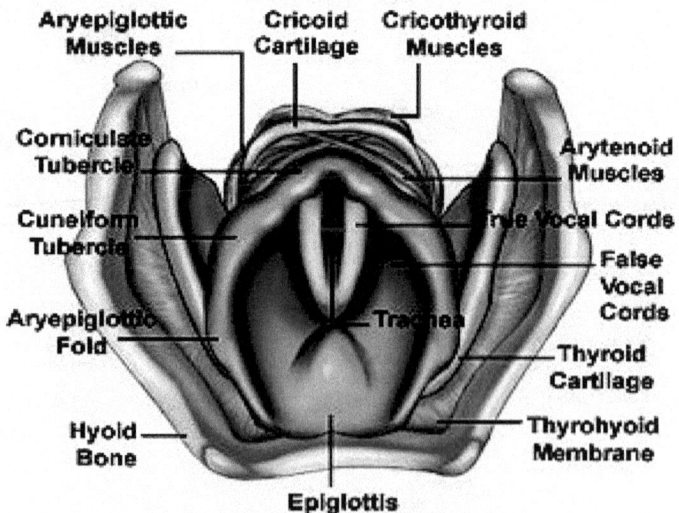

fig: 2.3 Larynx and Vocal Cords

attached to a small cartilage. Many small muscles are also attached to this cartilage. These muscles contract or relax during the various stages of breathing, swallowing, and speaking, and their action is vital to the normal function of the larynx.

The vocal cords consist of two delicate ligaments, shaped like lips which open and close as air passes through them. One end is attached to a pair of movable cartilages called the arytenoids, while the other is firmly anchored to the thyroid cartilage which is part of the Adam's apple. The arytenoid cartilages alter position so that the space between the cords i.e. glottis varies in shape from a wide V during speech to a closed slit during swallowing. Glottis is an opening between the two vocal cords. The glottis opens during breathing and closes during swallowing and sound production. The vibration of the vocal

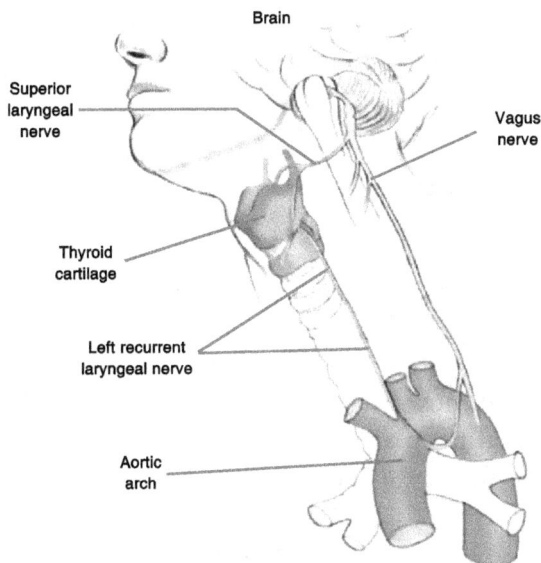

The brain coordinates voice production through specific nerve connections and signals. Signals to the voice box for moving voice box muscles (motor nerves) come from motor branches of Recurrent Laryngeal Nerve (RLN) and the Superior Laryngeal Nerve (SLN). Signals from the voice box structures for feeling (sensory nerves) travel through sensory branches of the RLN and SLN.

fig: 2.4 Vagus Nerve

cords during speech occurs when the glottis narrows and air from the lungs is expelled over the cords and through the larynx. This is called phonation. **The loudness of the voice is controlled by the force with which the air is expelled and the pitch by the length and tension of the cords. The natural depth and timbre of the voice is due to the shape, size and health of the articulators like the throat, nose and mouth and the resonators.** This is why men, who generally have large larynxes and long, slack vocal cords, tend to have deeper voices than women, who generally have smaller larynxes than men.

Two branches of the vagus nerve provide control over these muscles : 1. The recurrent laryngeal nerve and 2. The superior laryngeal nerve (see fig. 2.4). These branches are vulnerable to injury due to trauma, surgery, or other causes. This may lead to hoarseness, aspiration, and other symptoms associated with laryngeal nerve injury or even to paralysis of the vocal cords.

The mouth is intimately involved in speech because it helps to shape sounds emanating from the voice box or larynx. Making the sounds of consonants such as K or T, for example, demands that the air coming from the larynx is cut off sharply by the tongue and palate, while vowel sounds such as A & E need no truncation i.e. cutting off, but certain positions of the tongue and teeth. **Each sound in any language is determined by a slightly different movement of the lips, tongue and teeth.** The ability of deaf people to lip-read is proof of the role which the mouth plays in the production of speech.

The vocal cords serve a function similar to that of the reed in a wind instrument such as a Shehnai or a trumpet. When a person blows air over the reed, the reed vibrates, producing the basic sound which is then modified by the size and holes of the instrument. Similarly, the vocal cords vibrate when someone vocalizes, and the sounds produced are modified by the throat, nose and mouth.

C. Producing Speech Sounds

1. Phonation

It is a complicated process in which sound is produced for speech. During phonation, the vocal cords are brought together near the centre of the larynx by muscles attached to the arytenoids. As air is forced through the vocal cords, they vibrate and produce sound. Contracting or relaxing the muscles of the arytenoids can alter the qualities of this sound. As the sound produced by the larynx travels through the throat and mouth, it is further modified to produce speech. Fig. 2.5 illustrates the position of the vocal cords during breathing and phonation, respectively.

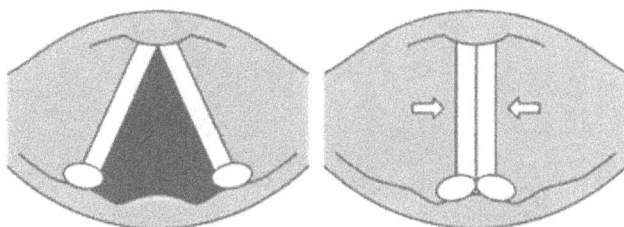

This figure illustrates two views of the vocal cords. On the left, the vocal cords are pulled laterally to open the glottis, such as when a person inhales, or takes a breath of air. On the right, the vocal cords are pulled towards the midline, to close the glottis, as when a person vocalizes or holds his breath.

fig: 2.5 Phonation and Vocal Cords

2. Production of Airflow

The lungs first supply adequate airflow to overcome the resistance of the closed vocal cords. The diaphragm, intercostal muscles and other chest muscles control the flow and pressure of air. **This control helps to regulate the delicate control over the voice, a must for all actors and singers. The vocal cords are finely tuned neuro-muscular units that adjust pitch and tone** by altering their position and tension.

3. Sound Production

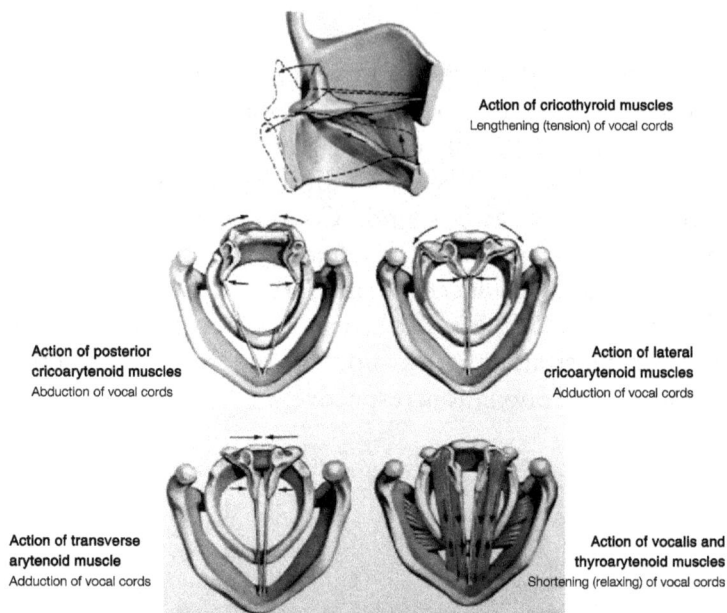

Action of cricothyroid muscles
Lengthening (tension) of vocal cords

Action of posterior
cricoarytenoid muscles
Abduction of vocal cords

Action of lateral
cricoarytenoid muscles
Adduction of vocal cords

Action of transverse
arytenoid muscle
Adduction of vocal cords

Action of vocalis and
thyroarytenoid muscles
Shortening (relaxing) of vocal cords

fig: 2.6 Sound Production

This diagram illustrates the vocal cord vibration cycle that occurs during sound production. The rapid opening and closing of the vocal cords occur in a vibratory pattern and are responsible for sound production. Thus any structural, inflammatory, or neoplastic lesion of the vocal cord affects voice production and quality.

4. Articulation of Voice

Articulation of voice is the process where the phonated sound is given meaning to vowel sounds from the vocal cords by pronouncing alphabets and words. This is done with the help of the articulators. All the organs which involve in the articulation process are called as articulators. Final modification of the voice occurs in the mouth or the oral cavity where the nose, throat, the tongue, palate, cheek and lips are involved in articulation (speech production).

To turn the simple sounds produced by the vocal cords into

intelligible words, the lips, the tongue, the soft palate and the chambers which give resonance to the voice all play a part. The resonating chambers include the whole mouth chamber, the nose, the pharynx (the part of the throat between the mouth and the esophagus), sinuses and to a lesser degree the chest cavity.

The control of these structures is achieved by hundreds of tiny muscles which work very closely together and at incredible speed. **In other words, speech is made up of vowels and consonants – vowels are all phonated sounds.**

The resonant qualities of the various chambers of the mouth and respiratory system provide us with the individuality of our voices called as timbre. For instance, the so called 'nasal sounds' like m, n and ng depend for their correct vocalization on free resonance in the nose; if we pinch our nose when we say something – the comic effect shows how the air space of the nose gives our speech roundness and clarity. **Different people have different shapes of nose, chest and mouth; hence different people have different timbre, the sounding quality of the voices.**

The skull also resonates when we speak, and we hear part of what we say transmitted through the bones of the skull, as well as what is picked up by the ears. This not only provides us with vital 'feedback' about what we are saying, but also explains why our voices sound so strange when played back through a tape recorder – the sounds we then hear being only those transmitted through air.

D. Registers

Voice registers correspond to differences in tone caused by different adjustments of the larynx. Two ("heavy" and "light") or three ("chest", "middle or throat", and "head") registers are commonly identified.

In the heavy or chest voice, the thyro-arytenoid muscles are active and hence shortened. The crico-thyroid muscles are passive in this register.

As the pitch rises, the crico-thyroid muscles contract and apply tension to the vocal cords. At the same time, however, the thyro-arytenoid muscles engage and thicken the vocal cords. Experienced speakers/singers learn to control both muscle sets to avoid "cracking" an involuntary head tone. This is throat or middle register where crico-thyroid and thyro-arytenoid muscles are approximately in equal activity.

In the light or head register, the thyro-arytenoid muscles are passive. In this state they offer little resistance to the crico-thyroid activity.

The voice of chest register has more of abdominal and chest resonance, containing more of lower harmonics, whereas the head register voice contains more of upper harmonics because of a lot of head resonance in it.

The concept of registers according to ancient Indian texts is given further in the next Chapter.

E. Ear

The corresponding sense organ of voice is the ear. In fig. 2.7, we can see the ear diagram, which is explained further.

Ear is a complex organ that is divided into three parts: the outer ear, which gathers sound like a radar scanner; the middle ear, whose gear-like assembly of bones amplify the sounds they receive; and the inner ear, which converts sound vibrations into electrical impulses and works out the position of the head.

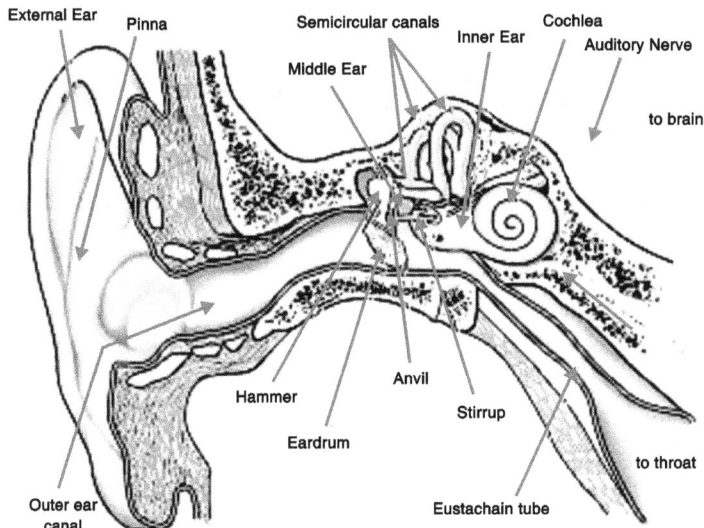

fig: 2.7 Ear

1. External Ear

i. Pinna

Pinna is also called as Auricle. It is the visible part of the outer ear. It collects sound and directs it into the outer ear canal.

ii. Outer ear canal

It is the tube through which sound travels to the eardrum.

2. Middle Ear

i. Eardrum

It is also called as Tympanic Membrane, a thin membrane that vibrates when sound waves reach it.

ii. Hammer

It is also called Malleus, a tiny bone that passes vibrations from the eardrum to the anvil.

iii. Anvil

Also called as Incus, it is a tiny bone that passes vibrations from the hammer to the Stirrup.

iv. Stirrup

Another name for Stirrup is Stapes. It is a tiny, U-shaped bone that passes vibrations from Anvil to Cochlea.

3. Inner Ear
i. Cochlea
It is a spiral-shaped, fluid-filled inner ear structure; it is lined with cilia (tiny hairs) that move when vibrated and cause a nerve impulse to form.. It houses the organ of Corti, which contains the 13,000 hair cells which are designed to receive the acoustic energy.
ii. Eustachian tube
This is a tube that connects the middle ear to the back of the nose; it equalizes the pressure between the middle ear and the air outside.
iii. Nerves
These nerves carry electro-chemical signals from the inner ear (the cochlea) to the temporal lobe of the brain.
iv. Semicircular canals
These are three loops of fluid-filled tubes that are attached to the cochlea in the inner ear. They help us maintain our sense of balance.

4. Hearing
Sound is collected by the Pinna (the visible part of the ear) and directed through the outer ear canal. The sound makes the eardrum vibrate, which in turn causes a series of three tiny bones (the hammer, the anvil, and the stirrup) in the middle ear to vibrate. The vibration is transferred to the snail-shaped cochlea in the inner ear. The cochlea is lined with sensitive hairs, which trigger the generation of nerve signals that are sent to the brain. The resulting messages are transmitted to the brain along a pair of nerves which lie side by side: the vestibular nerve for balance and the cochleal nerve for sound. The outer and middle ears are concerned mainly with hearing. The inner ear structures which interpret head position and sound are separate. The sound impressions are received and interpreted by the brain in the auditory cortex, situated in the temporal lobe.

As the sound travels from the Outer Ear to the Inner Ear, the sound pressure increases as the passage narrows down. The surface area of the eardrum is large (about 85 sq mm) and the surface area of the base of the stirrup is very small (about 3.2 sq mm). The pressure increases approximately 17 times as a result of differences in surface areas and sizes.

There are approximately 30,000 neurons along the organ of Corti. The auditory signal then travels to the cerebellum where it divides, half crossing over to the other side. Each half nerve ends in the temporal lobe of the brain, i.e. input from each ear ends up in the brain on both sides of the brain. This nerve impulse transforms of the acoustical signal into electrical energy.

The ear not only provides us with our sense of hearing, it also gives us the sense of balance.

We hear sound waves which are produced by the vibrations of air molecules, the size and energy of these waves determines loudness, which is measured in decibels (dB). The threshold of pain is 100 to 120 dB, whereas, the danger zone of hearing loss starts at 85 dB. The number of vibrations or cycles per second is called as frequency - more the vibrations, higher the pitch of the sound. Sound frequency is expressed in terms of cycles per second, or hertz (Hz).

In young persons, the range of audible frequencies is approximately 20 to 20,000Hz per second, though the ear is most sensitive to sounds in the middle range of 500 to 4,000Hz. As we get older, or if we are exposed to excessively loud noise over a period of time, our hearing becomes less acute in the higher frequencies. In order to measure the extent of hearing loss, normal hearing levels are defined as per the international standard. A person's level of hearing is the difference in decibels between the faintest pure note perceived, and the standard note generated by a special machine called Audiometer.

The ear acts as a receiver (outer ear), an amplifier (middle ear) and a transmitter (inner ear).

Changes in the pitch or loudness of sounds are sensed by tiny hairs on the basilar membrane through pressure waves transmitted in the fluid passing up and down the length of the cochlea. The cochlea nerve runs to a specialized part of the brain called the auditory or hearing centre.

The way in which waves are turned into electrical energy and interpreted by the brain is not understood. The current theory is that the cells of the cochlea measure pressure waves in the fluid and turn them into electrical impulses. It is also not clear how the ear distinguishes between loudness and pitch.

F. Respiratory System

Oxygen is the single most important substance on which our lives depend. It is essential to every cell and tissue in the body, which uses the Oxygen to produce energy necessary to support life. Oxygen is brought into the body when we inhale and its by-products are given off when we exhale. This process of

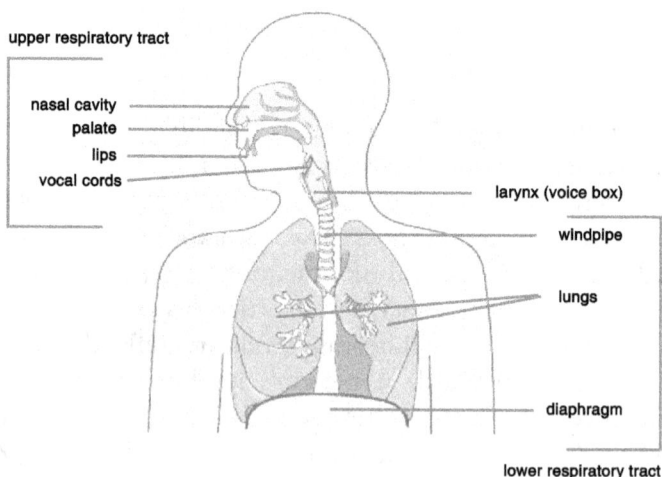

fig: 2.8 Respiratory System

respiration involves diaphragm, the upper respiratory tract – the nasal cavity, pharynx, larynx, and lower respiratory tract - trachea, primary bronchii and lungs (see fig.2.8). The pharynx and larynx together are termed as throat in our colloquial language.

1. The Nasal Cavity
Apart from being the organ of smell, the nose is the natural pathway by which air enters the body in the normal course of breathing. In addition, it acts as a protective device against irritants such as dust, which are usually expelled by sneezing and therefore do not have a chance to damage the lungs. The sinuses – spaces in the front of the skull – are connected with the inside of the nose. They are located behind the eyebrows and behind the cheeks, in the triangle between the eyes and the nose. Sinuses will help cushion the impact of any blows to the face. As an organ of Voice, the nose acts as resonator, richening the voice with upper harmonics and overtones.

2. The Throat
Throat is a term popularly used to describe the area that leads into the respiratory and digestive tracts. It is usually considered to extend from the oral and nasal cavities to the esophagus and trachea. Anatomically, this area is described as two separate parts, the pharynx and the larynx. Here it will be considered as the larynx, pharynx and trachea, which, together with the nose and mouth form the upper respiratory tracts.

3. Larynx
This is a respiratory as well as voice organ too. Its respiratory importance and functions have also been explained earlier along with the voice functions..

4. The Pharynx
The pharynx is the area at the back of the mouth, extending a little way down inside the neck. Deeply lined with muscles, it is

shaped, very roughly, like an inverted cone, extending for about 12cm behind the arch at the back of the mouth where it joins up with the gullet or esophagus.

The upper part of the pharynx is given rigidity by the bones of the skull, while at the lower end its muscles are joined to the elastic cartilages of the voice box or larynx. The outermost tissue layer of the pharynx, continuous with the lining of the mouth, contains many mucus-producing glands which help to keep the mouth and throat well lubricated during eating and speaking.

Anatomically, the pharynx is divided into three sections according to their positions and the jobs, each is designed to perform.

i. The uppermost part, the nasopharynx, gets its name from the fact that it lies above the level of the soft palate and forms the back of the nose.

ii. The part of the pharynx at the back of the mouth, called as oropharynx. This is the airway between mouth and lungs. Oropharynx is much more mobile than the nasopharynx. The squeezing actions of the muscles of the oropharynx help shape the sounds of speech as they come from the larynx. The most important organs of the oropharynx are the tonsils, tissues which are often implicated in the sore throats common in childhood.

iii. The lowermost or laryngeal section of the pharynx which is involved entirely with swallowing is called as laryngeopharynx. This is an important organ involved in the timbre of our voice.

5. The Trachea

The upper part of the trachea is at the front of the throat and consists of hoops of cartilage that hold open elastic tissue. We can feel this part of the trachea quite easily with our fingers through the skin at the base of the neck. At the upper part of the neck, the trachea is covered by the thyroid cartilage, or Adam's apple. From here the trachea divides itself in two main branches called as Bronchi, one each extending to both lungs. The trachea, like the nose, is lined with a mucous membrane that contains cells, which waft invading germs and dust back up into the throat to be swallowed.

6. The Lungs

The two lungs fill most of the thorax. The right is larger than the left as the heart takes up more room on the left side of the thorax. Each lung is divided into lobes; the right lung has three lobes, upper, middle and lower, and the left lung has two upper and lower. The lobes are separate from one another and marked by grooves on the surface-fissures.

The lungs themselves have a dense latticework of tubes. The largest of these are the **bronchi**, which, at the top of the lungs, divide off from the trachea to the left and right, each entering its respective lung. Inside the lung the bronchi branch out into secondary and tertiary (third) bronchi, and these branch further into smaller tubes called **bronchioles.** The bronchioles terminate in air sacs called **alveoli.**

i. Breathing Capacity:
a. Total Lung Capacity

It is the maximum air which can at any time be held in the two lungs. A normal human adult's total lung capacity is around 6000 ml.

Table of Respiratory Volumes

	Tidal Volume (Breathing Capacity)	Alveolar Air	350		
Vital Capacity		Dead Air Space	150	500	4500
	Inspiratory Reserve Volume			3000	
	Expiratory Reserve Volume			1000	
Residual Air					1500
Total Lung Capacity					**6000**

chart 2:2

Chapter II
Anatomy and Physiology of Voice

b. Residual Air

Some air is always left in the lungs even after forcibly breathing out. This left-over (residual) air is about 1500 ml.

c. Tidal Volume

It is 500 ml. which is the air breathed in and out in a normal quiet breathing. It is the total of dead air space and alveolar air.

d. Dead Air Space

The tidal air that is left in the respiratory passages where no diffusion of gases can occur is 150 ml.

e. Alveolar Air

Remaining tidal air in the air sacs is around 350 ml.

f. Expiratory Reserve Volume is the air that can be expelled forcibly after an ordinary expiration (also called as supplemental air). It is normally 1000 ml.

g. Inspiratory Reserve Volume is the air that can be drawn in forcibly over and above the tidal air (also called as complemental air). It is normally 3000 ml.

h. Vital Capacity

It is 4500 ml. which is the volume of air that can be taken in and expelled by maximum inspiration and expiration.

When we say, that there is an increase in the breathing capacity, it is the Optimal Breathing Capacity we increase. It is the Tidal volume plus the active capacity of the reserve volumes, used whenever needed during physical activities. It should not be mistaken as Total Lung Capacity, which cannot be changed. During normal breathing we use the Tidal Volume. But, when we do physical activity we use the active air sacs in the reserve volumes, as much as the need arises. When we say that the Optimal Volume increases it is a combination of increase in the Tidal Volume and the capacity to use more and more of the Alveolar Air or using more and more air sacs during breathing.

The Total Lung Capacity varies from person to person according to the structural volume of lungs.

ii. Breath Control:

Breath Control is the control of breathing movements. They are largely controlled by a respiratory centre located in the Medulla Oblongata of the brain. This centre is stimulated by the carbon dioxide content of the blood. More the carbon dioxide content in the blood, faster is the breathing. These breathing movements are normally not under the control of the will, i.e. they are involuntary movements. But, to a large extent, we can consciously increase or decrease the rate and extent of breathing. It is possible to consciously train the breathing muscles and gain a control over its movements to develop good singing. This process of developing the control is called as pranayaam in Yoga Practice.

7. Diaphragm:

It is a dome shaped thick sheet of muscular tissue separating the thorax and abdomen. It tapers near the lungs. The breathing movements of the diaphragm are controlled by the medulla oblongata. It is the medulla oblongata that sends impulses to the diaphragm to contract and expand. This creates increase and decrease in sizes of the chest and the changes in the pressure in the lung cavities, which makes

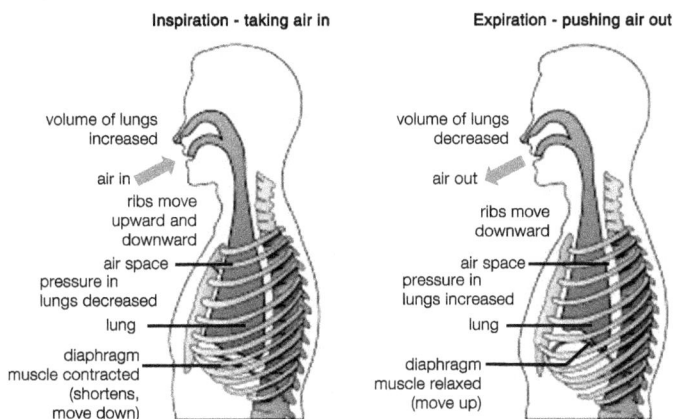

fig. 2.9 Diaphragm Positions During Breathing

respiration possible. A control of the movements of the diaphragm is important to a speaker/singer. During inhalation the diaphragm contracts i.e. moves down and during exhalation it comes to its normal position by moving up. (see fig.2.9)

G. Brain

The brain is the main switching unit of the central nervous system; it is the place to which impulses flow and from which impulses originate. The spinal cord provides the link between the brain and the rest of the body. The brain is a highly organized organ that contains approximately 100 billion neurons and has a mass of 1.4 kilograms. Let us see the functions of the brain more elaborately.

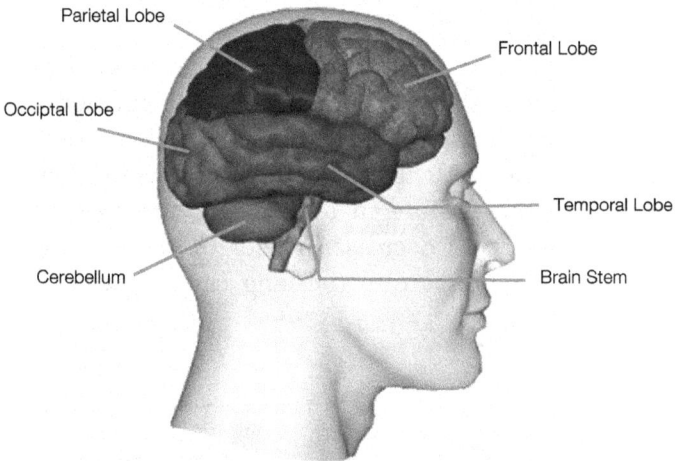

fig: 2.10 Parts of the Brain

1. Cerebrum:
Cerebrum is the seat of intelligence, consciousness and will power. It controls all the voluntary actions. What is generally called as the subconscious and the unconscious mind is also located in the Cerebrum. (see fig.2.10)

i. Frontal Lobe of the Cerebrum

It is the top, front regions of each of the cerebral hemispheres. They are used for reasoning, emotions, judgment, and voluntary movement. Front part of the brain; involved in planning, organizing, problem solving, selective attention, complicated thinking, planning of speech or singing, personality development and a variety of "higher cognitive functions" including behavior and emotions.

ii. Parietal Lobe of the Cerebrum

Parietal Lobe is the middle lobe of each cerebral hemisphere between the frontal and occipital lobes. It contains important sensory centres (located at the upper rear of the head). It contains the sensory area for touch. (for details see fig.2.15)

iii. Temporal Lobe of the Cerebrum

It is the region at the lower side of each cerebral hemisphere (see fig.2.10 and 2.11); contains centres of hearing and memory (located at the sides of the head). They sort one sound from the other and are responsible for visual (right lobe) and verbal (left lobe) memory. This lobe also contains the sensory areas of taste and smell.

Broca's Area and Wernicke's Area – Areas of the Temporal Lobe -

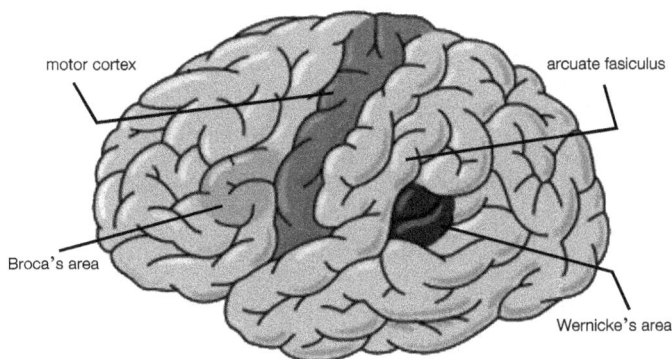

fig:2.11 Broca's area and Wernicke's area

They are located in the lower part of the (left) brain (see fig.2.11). Broca's area is thought to be responsible for speech, language planning, sequencing, and production. Wernicke's area is thought to be responsible for understanding language. Broca's area and Wernicke's area are connected by a bundle of nerve fibers called the arcuate fasiculus.

iv. Occipital Lobe of the Cerebrum
This is the region at the back of each cerebral hemisphere that contains the centres of vision and reading ability (located at the back of the head).

Speaking Written and Heard Word

Speaking the Written Word	Speaking the Heard Word
motor cortex, arcuate fasiculus, Broca's area, Wernicke's area, Primary Visual Cortex	motor cortex, arcuate fasiculus, Broca's area, Primary Auditory Cortex, Wernicke's area
To speak a word that is read, information must first get to the primary visual cortex. From the primary visual cortex, information is transmitted to the posterior speech area, including Wernicke's area. From Wernicke's area, information travels to Broca's area, then to the Primary Motor Cortex.	To speak a word that is heard, information must first get to the primary auditory cortex. From the primary auditory cortex, information is transmitted to the posterior speech area, including Wernicke's area. From Wernicke's area, information travels to Broca's area, then to the Primary Motor Cortex.

chart shows the process of speaking a read word and the process of imitating a heard word. We can see that the initial visual and auditory reception is done by different parts of the brain. This can explain why some persons find it difficult to understand a script or the music notations. Reading language/music and understanding language/music are different concepts and need to be studied differently.

chart 2:3

2. Cerebellum
This is the part of brain below the back of the cerebrum. It regulates body balance, posture, movement, muscle

coordination and fast muscle movements. If it does not function properly, coordination of muscle movements or quick tempo speaking/singing is not possible i.e. a speaker/singer may speak/sing clumsily, full of mistakes or find difficulty in adjusting the voice for the required pitch.

3. Brain Stem
It is a complex network of wiring for sensory and muscle nerves. Functions of the brain stem are controlling eye movements, breathing, heart rate, arousal and consciousness, sleep and wake cycles and attention and concentration.

i. Pons
It is the part of the Brain Stem that joins the hemispheres of the Cerebellum and connects the Cerebrum with the Cerebellum. It is located just above the Medulla Oblongata. It carries impulses from one hemisphere of the cerebellum to the other and coordinates the muscular movements of both the sides.

ii. Medulla Oblongata
It is the lowest section of the brainstem (at the top end of the spinal cord). It function is to control the involuntary activities of the internal organs including movement of the alimentary canal, heartbeat, breathing etc.

4. Corpus Collosum
It is a large bundle of nerve fibers that connects the left and right cerebral hemispheres. In the lateral section, it looks a bit

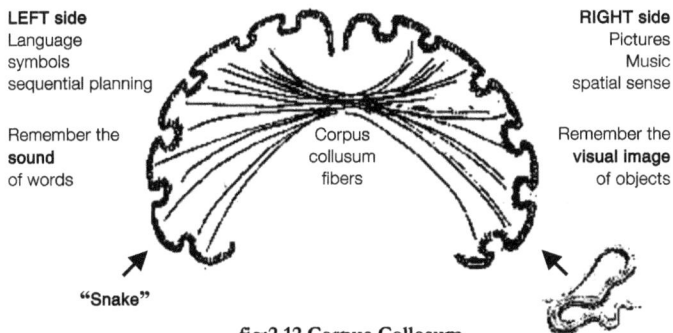

fig:2.12 Corpus Collosum

like "C" on its side. In fig.2.12 we can see that the signals and interpretations from the left and right brain are coordinated to make sense of what is seen or heard.

5. Spinal Cord

It is a thick bundle of nerve fibers that runs from the base of the brain to the hip area, running through the spine (vertebrae). It sends to the brain motor impulses from the trunk and limbs. It also sends sensory impulses from the brain to the trunk and limbs.

6. Paranasal Sinuses

These are lined cavities in specific bones. These air spaces are lined with a mucus membrane. They're found in the Frontal, Ethmoid, Sphenoid, and Maxillary bones. They serve to decrease the weight of the skull and to function as resonators for the voice. These resonators add the upper harmonics and overtones to our voice. In fig2.13 we can view the sinuses from the front and side.

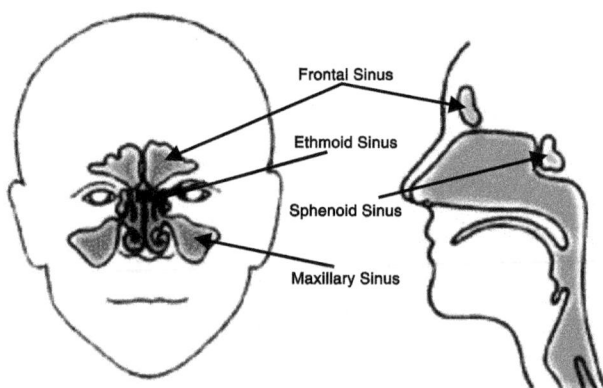

fig:2.13 Paranasal Sinuses

7. The Cortex

It is a layer which has the thickness of an orange peel, and is the actual area where most "thinking" takes place (see fig.2.14). The cortex has many specialized patches. It can be also thought of as the "unconscious mind" because most patches of the cortex work automatically. For example, our sensory areas work 24 hours a day, monitoring incoming sounds and skin signals (our vision areas don't get signals at night, so we use dreams to keep them active).

8. Association fibers

They carry information from one patch of the cortex to another. The vision areas will process what comes from the eye to see lines and shapes, then pass it on to area which determines distance and motion, and further to area which is designed to recognize objects.

9. Thalamus

It is the master control centre of the brain. It acts a Chief Executive Officer or CEO of the brain, monitoring all senses and actions.

10. The Limbic System

It is important for memory. For example, it can add "emotional tags" of "danger" to memories of snakes as shown in fig.2.12

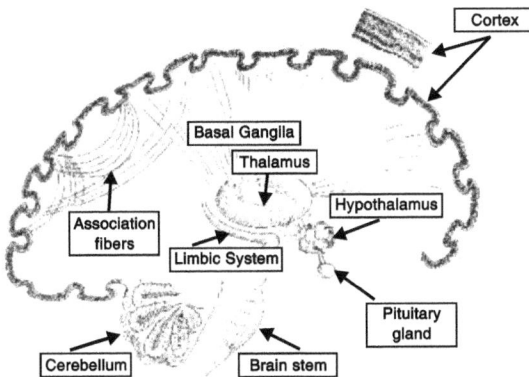

Inner Parts of the Brain

fig:2.14

11. The Hypothalamus

It is the master centre for emotions and instincts, such as

hunger, thirst, pleasure and anger. It also regulates our body temperature.

12. The Pituitary Gland

It translates nerve signals into chemical signals. Fear emotions in the hypothalamus can trigger the pituitary gland to produce hormones, the chemical messengers, to prepare the body for "fight or flight."

13. The Basal Ganglia

It is a network of nerve connections around the thalamus. It is like a gateway with a guard. For example, the "yes" area of our frontal lobe may want us to grab the sandwich off our friend's plate, while the "no" area tries to inhibit the action. The thalamus "conscious centre" or "will power" responds to whichever signal is stronger and controls the muscle signals via the basal ganglia, a 'go/stop' effect.

H. The Right and Left Brain

Our brain is made up of two halves, a left brain and a right brain. There's a big fold that goes from front to back in our brain, essentially dividing it into two distinct and separate parts. They are connected to each other the corpus collosum. The left side of our body is governed by the right side of our brain, and vice versa. It applies even to our eyes and ears, which process a majority of their sensory data on opposite sides of the brain.

The two brains function totally differently. They have opposite functions to perform and they see and understand the world differently. Usually a person is dominated by one brain. Skilful training can enhance the ability to balance the working of the two halves of the brain. This coordination ability is the key to superior intellectual abilities, where yoga can play an important role.

It is possible that a person can understand music but cannot sing, if his left brain is not trained or is not functioning properly.

Table showing the functions of the Left and Right Brain

LEFT BRAIN FUNCTIONS	RIGHT BRAIN FUNCTIONS
Logical	Creative
Words and Languages	Pictures and images
Math and Science	Philosophy and Religion
Ordered or Patterned Perception	Spatial Perception
Practical	Emotional
Present and Past	Present and Future
Arithmetic	Geometric
Secured	Risk Taking
Doubting	Believing, Trusting
Rational	Irrational
Rhythm	Tempo
Pitch	Scale, Musical Interval
Melody	Harmony, Chords
Language Memory	Musical Memory and Visual Memory
Part	Whole
Objective	Subjective
Analytical	Synthesizing

chart 2.4

Similarly, if the right brain is not functioning properly, it is possible that people cannot understand or learn music but are able to sing naturally. A person may be able to read words or music but cannot speak or sing and vice versa.

In fig 2.15 we can see the different functions of the two brains. The areas of delegation of work are well managed.

Now, let us consider the Role of the Brain. Speech, singing and its associated functions are usually concentrated in the left hemisphere. These areas of the brain (Broca's Area and Wernicke's Area) are connected to the motor speech centre which controls the muscles of the mouth and throat, and the sensory speech centre which interprets the incoming sound signals coming along the nerves from the ears. Also nearby are the parts of the brain which coordinate hearing (by which we comprehend what others around us are saying), vision (by which we decipher the written words) and the complex hand movements used in writing, playing instruments and so on.

Conversation and Singing is still more a very complicated procedure, and the first thing that happens when we hear a person speaking/singing is that the hearing centres, in the cerebral cortex, recognize the jumble of incoming auditory

Left Brain

Symbols
Math Symbols **1**
Match Body to Left and Right
Reading Clocks, etc.

Body Senses Right Side
a.Genitals, b.Foot, c.Leg
d.Trunk, e.Arm, f.Fingers
g.Face, h.Lips **2**

Grammar **3**
Spatial Arrangement of
Language

Spelling, Phonics, Reading
Matching Vision of Words **4**
with Sounds of Letters

Vision of Alphabet
a.from Eye Lines, Angles
b.Perceive Letter Shapes **5**
c.Recogonising Letters and Groups

Muscle Coordination
Speed of Repetitive Action
Balance **6**

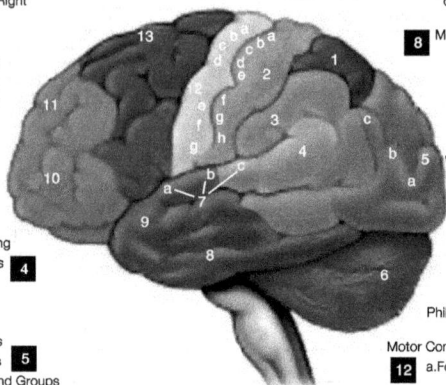

7 Sounds of Languages
a.Frequencies (from ear), b.Phonemes
c.Recognize Word Sounds

8 Memory, Language Memory
Stories, Face Names

9 Emotional Memory
Emotions and Language

Inhibition to say 'No'
What not to say, worrying,
10 talking to yourself
of what not to do

Imagination, Creativity
To say 'Yes', Create New
Patterns of Ideas and
11 Language, Writer,
Philosopher Impulsive Talking

Motor Control Muscles of Right Side
12 a.Foot, b.Leg, c.Trunk, d.Arm
e.Face, f.Lips, g.Tongue

Premotor Sequential Thinking
13 Takes Ideas, Actions, and Words
and puts them into Linear Sequence.

Right Brain

Spatial Sense
Mental Math, Body 3D Awareness
Touch 3D Recognition **1**
Object 3D Rotation
Construction, Navigation

Body Senses of
Left Side **2**
a.Genitals, b.Foot
c.Leg, d.Trunk, e.Arm
f.Fingers, g.Face, h.Lips

Vision
a.From Eye, Lines
and Angles **3**
b.Distance, Motion, Shape
c.Object Recognition

Music
a.Harmony (Spatial)
b.Musical Intervals **4**
c.Pitch (from ear)

Memory
a.Music, Audio Memory
b.Visual Memory
c.Face Memory **5**
d.Emotional memory feelings, fears, humour

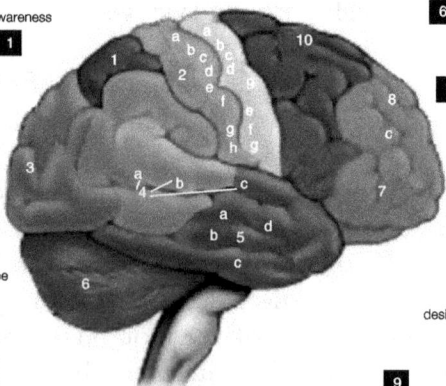

6 Muscle Coordination,
Speed of Repetitive
Action, balance

7 Inhibitions to say 'No'
What not to do,
Right-Wrong Behavior,
Manners, Conscience

Imagination,
8 Creativity, to say
'Yes' Create new
patterns of behaviour,
art, music, actions,
designs, etc. Impulsive Action

9 Motor Control of Left Side
a.Foot, b.Leg, c.Trunk, d.Arm
e.Face, f.Lips, g.Tongue

10 Premotor Learn how to do things
play sports, musical instruments habits

fig:2.15 Left and Right Brain Functions

signals from the ears. The sensory speech centre decodes the words, pitch, timbre, tempo, intensity, etc. so that the other parts of the brain involved in the process, can then recognize the words/music and formulate an answer or prepare to imitate it. Once this has been thought out, the motor speech centre and the brain stem come into operation. The brain stem controls both the intercostal muscles, between the ribs, which inflate the lungs, and the abdominal muscles which determine the pressure of the incoming and outgoing air. As air is expelled from the lungs, the motor speech areas signal the vocal cords simultaneously to move into the stream of air in the throat, causing the cords to vibrate and produce a simple sound.

The amount of pressure applied to the lungs during exhalation governs the speed with which the air passes over the vocal cords. Faster the air louder will be the sound produced. During whispering, the vocal cords are set wide apart so that they do not actually vibrate as the air passes between them, they merely act as friction surfaces. But for the most part, the shaping of words is performed by movements of the lips, tongue and soft palate, controlled by the cortex. **The pitch is decided by the vocal cords, intensity by the exerted breath pressure and timbre by the articulators and involuntarily by the resonators.**

I. Coordination

The musical rendering as well as speech activities of people reveal in their movements, how delicately the human brain can control the hundreds of action in such short time. To achieve such intricate and delicate sequences of action, the human brain has evolved a complex system of control and guidance, which makes even our advanced, sophisticated super computers look primitive.

A child is born with many reflexes. Reflexes of a child and that of an adult are quite different. This happens as the brain is trained to react differently for certain reflexes. Let us see an example of these reflexes in an adult, think how quickly you would withdraw you hand from a hot pan! But, a trained cook can touch or even hold hot pans easily. For every action we perform, some muscles will contract; others relax and still more maintain their contraction to stabilize the rest of the body. The process, by which all the individual muscle contractions are synchronized by the brain to produce a smooth order of activity, is called coordination. Training can improve this coordination.

1. How Coordination Works

To understand this, it is best to take an everyday action, such as leaning over a table to switch on the radio. How does the brain direct this apparently simple task? Before the radio can be switched on, a series of events must happen.

First, we must 'know' where the radio and our hand are, and the relationship between them. This means that our brain must be able to generate a 'map' of the outside space for the necessary movement to be planned. This is called spatial perception.

This map of the outside world must then be interpreted by the brain, so that the problem of switching on the radio which is on the table, by our hand can be solved. This plan of action must then be translated into a detailed set of instructions which is given to the muscles, so that they will contract in the right order.

During the movement started by the planning parts of the brain, continuous streams of information are pouring in and out from all the sensors (nerves) in the muscles and joints as to their position and state of contraction. All this information has to be organized and relayed back, to keep the map updated at every point of action and to make any adjustments which then becomes necessary.

Brain Parts Regulating Coordination

Brain Part	Coordination Function
Pons	Connects Cerebrum and Cerebellum, Muscular Movements
Medulla Oblongata	Involuntary Functions, Breathing
Corpus Collosum	Interpretation, Coordination of sound, pictures, space with language, symbols, sequence, etc.
Association Fibres	Coordination and Interpretation of information connected with thinking, supports Cortex activities of regulation of articulation
Thalmus	Master Coordinator
Limbic System	Coordination of emotions with memory
Pituitary Gland	Coverts Nerve impulses to chemical signals
Basal Ganglia	Network of nerve connections supporting Thalmus
Cerebellum	Muscle coordination, balance, speed
Cerebrum	Voluntary, willful - sensory and motor functions

These brain parts are responsible for the coordination
of sense organs and motor organs, left and
right brain activities, brain and body movements, etc.

chart 2:5

In order to move our hand to switch on the radio, we also need to lean slightly towards it. This alters the centre of gravity in your body. All the reflex balance mechanisms must be controlled to ensure that the correct changes in muscles tone are made, allowing the movement across the table that our brain has ordered. This means that the background tone of many other muscles has to be monitored and coordinated.

In this simple action of one second, thousands of actions have been coordinated by the brain at uncountable speed. Practically, all the parts of the brain are put to work in even this simple action.

2. First stages of coordination

All intentional movements need practice and training before they become coordinated. (In the example of switching on the radio, a child is unable to perform the action, but training itself by natural instinct and imitation, the child learns to coordinate the required actions by the age of 14-18 months.) Even such ordinary actions like interpreting the direction of the heard sound, were once major motor problems for every developing child. As a baby's brain matures and its interconnections increase, the primitive reflexes with which it was born (such as the 'startle' reaction, causing the hands to be out-stretched) are overlaid with progressively more complicated ways of moving.

These arrive as a result of the child's increasing senses. A toy might attract its eye, because its bright colour causes a strong signal in the child's visual centres, but the baby finds that reaching out is not enough to get hold of this object, so it is impelled to move towards it. The first attempts to move are not coordinated; the limbs simply thrash about wildly. But these enable the necessary brain connections to develop for the set of actions that make up a coordinated crawl. Once crawling has been achieved, the messages sent from the brain to the muscles can be improved upon until nothing at ground level is safe from the child's grasp.

When the baby discovers that it can pull itself into an upright position, the cerebellum has to analyze a new set of information coming from the balance centres in the brain stem. Walking is another new skill to learn, requiring many attempts during which the cerebellum co-operates with the motor cortex to develop efficient 'tunes' to play on the muscles.

The separate parts of each action learnt in this way are pre-programmed into the spinal cord, but they must form a coherent pattern to produce a coordinated movement, in the same way that an orchestra must have a conductor before it can produce a tuneful sound from the concerted action of all its instruments.

Once these relatively simple skills have been perfected, the brain has been so well programmed that no concentration is necessary – **the premotor cortex** says 'speak' and the right set of instructions go into action to produce the very complicated mechanical actions that are involved. The **cerebellum** monitors the progress of the action, but this becomes less and less a conscious event over a period. If a problem is introduced into the system, such as the change in the posture of the neck that is caused by microphones placed far from the mouth, some reprogramming is necessary and concentration needed whilst the motor cortex is instructed in this new 'tune'.

3. Advanced Coordination
This involves the coordination of all the sensory, receiving and interpreting centres of the brain and then with the movement of the rest of the body governed by the motor areas of the brain.

It is evident that this type of coordination, using most of the brain, is the last to mature. It forms the basis of learning the complex movements that are needed in various skills, such as voice modulations, playing a musical instrument, singing, reading music, learning a language, learning to write or read, etc.

When we understand the coordination processes of different actions, it becomes easier to understand that each type of action needs different coordination skills. Different parts of the brain are required to function by different actions. These actions are a series of continuous and complex coordinated flow of actions of the sensory and motor nerves of the brain. Hence, as introduced in Chapter 1, the brain parts to be coordinated for learning, performing, teaching and writing/composing will be different. Similarly, Understanding, Reading and Writing words/music need different types of coordination. Again understanding, performing, teaching, etc. need different perspectives to be developed in melody and harmony. A person may possess any one, or different permutations and combinations of all these skills. It is possible that a person may develop all these skills together.

Though speaking/singing activity is directly not related with the other senses except hearing, indirectly all the senses coordinate with each other to give the best expected results. Though auditory reception, understanding and memorizing are the most important factors, it is worth noting that we learn most of the things by the 'theory of association'. All the five senses work with coordination to store and memorize anything. We associate different sounds, languages, dictions, pitches, intensities, tempos, songs, raga-s, tala-s, etc. with different incidents, emotions, persons, etc. We experience that different incidents remind us of different words, speeches, raga-s or songs. Similarly certain words, phrases or songs trigger certain memories, so on and so forth. For any speaking/singing activity the whole brain plays a very important role.

In performance, teaching and composing, not only language or musical learning but, any type and subject of learning are important. All information received from all the five senses is received by the brain. During filtering and interpretation it uses the earlier stored information. That is why different persons interpret a single piece of information differently, giving importance to different aspects of the same piece of information. This interpreted information is stored at different places in the brain. Threads of association are also simultaneously developed. Emotional, sensual (relating to senses), intellectual and other types of tags or labels are given to the messages. eg. A particular phrase or song reminds us of particular incident in our life. The logical and the creative brain in the process of memorizing, scan all the gathered information of any and all subjects, for any type of its motor activity.

Some people's brains seem well equipped from birth to develop in particular way. However, to a large extent, the differences between people's abilities in complex types of coordination, depends on the depth of their desire and `will to learn and to the extent to which they can concentrate to build up these programmes.

As *yoga* is holistic in its approach, it works on this coordination very well. It helps in developing the higher brain functions. This functional ability is the uniqueness of *yoga*.

J. Yogic View of Anatomy and Physiology

Anatomy and physiology of the human body and mind have been known to yoga since vedic times. Yoga goes beyond the physical body and explains the science of 'soul' (*atman*) and its evolution and development. Ayurveda and Yoga are two closely related spiritual and sacred sciences rooted in the vedic tradition of India. Both disciplines have always been used together for better living, balancing of the body and mind and progress of the soul (*atman*). The anatomy and physiology explained by both the sciences have common principles and are holistic in nature. 'Yoga' deals with the science of life from the spiritual aspect and 'Ayurveda' talks about the science of life from the individual, social and routine health aspects. Their thinking pattern varies from their basic aspects and assumptions in comparison with contemporary medical sciences. Whereas modern medicine directs their goal towards physical and mental health, Yoga and Ayurveda direct their goal towards the health as well as conscious progress of the body, mind along with evolution of the soul (*atman*).

The next Chapter explains these terms, aspects and assumptions more elaborately.

Chapter III
Yoga for Singer

A. Meaning of Yoga

When we talk about Yoga in general, it is assumed that we are mentioning about Dhyana yoga.

Dhyana Yoga Practice is mainly divided into two streams:
1. Hathayoga, which mainly talks about Asana, Mudra, Bandha, Pranayam and Nadanusandhan, and
2. Patanjalyoga also known as Rajayoga, which talks about Dharana, Dhyana and Samadhi.

Hathayoga is the first step towards Rajayoga.

Kriya Yoga, Kundalini Yoga, Tantra, Laya Yoga, etc. are combinations of these Yoga streams or a more detailed learning of one or more aspects from them.

There are ample references of 'Yoga' in Upanishad-s. Rishi Yajnyavalkya (belonging to Ramayan period) has also stated about Yoga. But, the first systematic enunciation of Yoga goes to the credit of Maharshi Patanjali (around 2nd century B.C.). His treatise on Yoga is titled 'Patanjal Yogadarshan'. He explains Yoga as:

योगश्चित्तवृत्तिनिरोधः || १.०२ ||
yogashchittavrttinirodah || 1.02 ||

meaning: conscious restraint of the vibrations of the chitta
(subtlest part of the mind)

Patanjal Yogadarshan is also known as Indian Psychology. Rishi Vyas (of 1st century B.C.) is the first commentator of 'Yogadarshan'. He says,

योगः समाधिः | |

yogah samaadhihi | |

meaning: 'Yoga' means to go beyond mind towards the Ultimate Truth
i.e. to go in 'Samadhi'.

'Yoga' is derived from the Sanskrit verb 'Yuja', meaning 'to join'.

There are many explanations given by different sages, which lead to more or less similar understanding. We can say that the processes or paths of joining the individual soul (Jeevatma) with the cosmic soul (Paramatma) is termed as Yoga. **These paths as well as the ultimate goal, both are termed as 'Yoga'.**

Brahma is related to and compared to Nada in the Upanishads. Here nada means a vibratory form of the Brahma i.e. the Universe, the Cosmos. The purpose of yoga is to become one with the 'Nadabrahma', or go beyond duality.

When we go into the depths of its meaning we find that the boundaries of the word yoga expand having different aspects. Widely speaking, we can say that any path that takes us to the realms of 'moksha' or Self-realization is the path of yoga. So jnana, bhakti, dhyana, laya, nada, karma, tantra, etc. are all paths which take us to the same goal of Self realization. Moksha, Samadhi, Nirvana or Kaivalya are names of a similar state of consciousness. Hence all these goals are also called as Yoga in a broader sense.

This book discusses about the different yogic paths and their by-product benefits which help to improve our 'Holistic Voice'.

In the chapter of karmayoga from Bhagwat Geeta, yoga is explained as:

समत्वं योग उच्यते || २.४८ ||

samatvam yoga uchyate || 2.48 ||

meaning: yoga means a perfect balance of the intellect
i.e. intellectual balance between success & failure with non attachment
towards these consequences

योगः कर्मसु कौशलम् || २.५० ||

yogah karmasu koushalam || 2.50 ||

meaning: doing a karma (action) with awareness and balance of intellect
(i.e. doing a karma in a yogic way) is the greatest skill

B. Yogic View Of Cosmic Principles (tattwa-s).

Yoga has accepted the twenty five principles of Sankhya Philosophy. Out of twenty five there are two basic principles as 'Purusha' and 'Prakriti' and other twenty-three principles are the manifestation of 'Prakriti'. These twenty five principles are:

1. Purusha (Pure Consciousness):
It is the Ultimate principle encompassing the Universe. It is beyond all objectivity.

2. Prakriti (Primordial Nature):
It is the ultimate substance behind whatever that can be perceived. Prakriti is composed of three Guna-s (prime qualities):

i. Sattva (Balance), the quality of light, intelligence and illumination

ii. Rajas (Motion), the quality of energy, life and activity. The potentials that are already manifested at the time of our birth stay here. Of course they need further stimulation for flowering.

iii. Tamas (Resistance, Inertia), the quality of matter, passivity and a dwelling place of latent potentials

All the following principles contain all these three tattwa-s.

3. Mahat and Buddhi (Cosmic and Individual Intelligence):

It contains within itself all the laws of Nature. It is Prakriti in action. Buddhi is the individual manifestation of Mahat.

4. Ahankara (Cosmic and Individual Ego):

It is the basis of all multiplicity that occurs in the manifestation process of division. Prakriti creates the mind, five sense organs and five motor organs for working of Individual Ego.

5. Manas (Mind):

It coordinates the sense and motor activities through emotions, sensations and imagination. Its dominant qualities are Sattva and Rajas. Usually, the mind dominates in a layman's life.

6-10. Pancha Tanmatra-s (Five Potentials or Subtle Elements):

The three Guna-s which are only in the form of Casual Energy (energy containing a cause to manifest) or concept, give rise by their combination to five, very subtle levels of impressions called as Tanmatra-s. They are the root energies. The five Tanmatra-s are: Shabda, Sparsha, Roopa, Rasa, and Gandha. The Pancha Mahabhoota-s are derived from these Pancha Tanmatra-s.

11-15. Pancha Mahabhoota-s (Five Elements):

These are the manifested forms of the five Tanmatra-s. Each Tanmatra has a corresponding Mahabhoota, Jnanendriya and Karmendriya. (See chart 3.1)

16-20. Pancha Jnanendriya-s (Five Sense Organs):

The outer world is experienced through the sense organs. This perception is further collected and deciphered by the mind and analyzed by the Buddhi.

21-25. Pancha Karmendriya-s (Five Motor Organs):

Each sense organ has a respective motor organ, which is put to action by Buddhi through the mind.

Tanmatra-s, Mahabhoota-s, Jnanendriya-s and Karmendriya-s

Tanmatra (Subtle Elements)	Mahabhoota (Elements)	Jnanendriya (Sense Organs)	Karmendriya (Motor Organs)
Shabda (Sound, Word)	Akasha (Ether, Space)	Ears (Hearing)	Mouth (Voice)
Sparsha (Touch)	Vayu (Air)	Skin (Touch)	Hand
Roopa (Sight)	Teja, Agni (Fire)	Eyes (Seeing)	Feet
Rasa (Taste)	Aapa (Water)	Tongue (Taste)	Urino-Genitals
Gandha (Smell)	Prithvi (Earth)	Nose (Smell)	Anus

chart 3.1

The five Tanmatra-s have a specific method of derivation. The primary Tanmatra is 'Shabda' or sound. This Tanmatra further develops itself into 'Sparsha'. The Sparsha Tanmatra contains Shabda Tanmatra in it. Similarly, the Roopa Tanmatra is a further development of Sparsha Tanmatra, containing Shabda, Sparsha and Roopa Tanmatra-s in it. Similarly, the Rasa Tanmatra has Shabda plus Sparsha plus Roopa plus Rasa Tanmatra-s in it, and Gandha has all the five Tanmatra-s present in it. **So, we can see that 'Shabda' is the only Tanmatra present in all the five Tanmatra-s.** In other words 'Shabda' i.e. Sound or Word which is termed as 'Nada' by the Yogi-s, is the quality present in any and every thing in this Universe. This gives rise to the term 'Nadabrahma', which is used in the Upanishad-s. Thus,

Shabda

Sparsha = **Shabda** + Sparsha

Roopa = **Shabda** + Sparsha + Roopa

Rasa = **Shabda** + Sparsha + Roopa + Rasa

Gandha = **Shabda** + Sparsha + Roopa + Rasa + Gandha

'Aakash' Mahabhoota is present in all the five Mahabhoota-s.

Let us extend this fact to the aspect of all sense organs, the Jnanendriya-s to the storing and memorizing of sound by our brain. The senses of touch, seeing, taste and smell include the aspect of hearing in a subtle manner. Thus,

Hearing
Touch = **Hearing** + Touch
Seeing = **Hearing** + Touch + Seeing
Taste = **Hearing** + Touch + Seeing + Taste
Smell = **Hearing** + Touch + Seeing + Taste+ Smell

This is how sound is stored in the brain by sense of touch, seeing, taste and smell.

Similarly, this fact extends to the actions of all motor organs, the Karmendriya-s for voice production. The motor actions of hands, legs, Urino-Genitals and Anus include the aspect of voice in a subtle manner. i.e. these organs also speak in a subtle language. Thus,

Voice
Hands = **Voice** + Hands
Feet = **Voice** + Hands + Feet
Urino-Genitals = **Voice** + Hands + Feet + Urino-Genitals
Anus = **Voice** + Hands + Feet + Urino-Genitals + Anus

This is how all senses and all actions, both voluntary and involuntary have a hidden Voice in them. That is why they are equally important in voice production.

Yoga also discusses three more principles:
1. Ishwar (Cosmic Lord):
Ishwar is a Special Purusha untouched by misery, actions, their results and desires. It is infinite wisdom. Presence of Ishwar makes the Prakriti to loose its equilibrium and start manifesting. The Ishwar discussed by Yoga is a formless concept beyond the parameters of Time and Space.

2. Chitta:

The Manas, Buddhi (a lesser form of Mahat) and Ahankara work together on the platform called as 'Chitta'. It is the infinite storehouse of force in nature.

3. Prana (Life Force Energy):

It is the power, energy required in the manifestation and division of the 'Aakash' Mahabhoota. It is the manifesting power of the Universe.

Maharshi Patanjali also discusses about Omkar (The Cosmic Sound) and equates it with Ishwara. He says,

तस्य वाचकः प्रणवः || १.२७ ||
tasya vaachakah praNavah || 1.27 ||

meaning: Omkar is the Word used for the manifestation of Ishwara.

Omkar is discussed further in this Chapter.

Thus, there are twenty eight Principles (Tattwa-s) – Purusha, Prakriti (and its twenty three sub-principles), Ishwar, Chitta and Prana.

C. Five Sheaths or the Panch Kosha-s

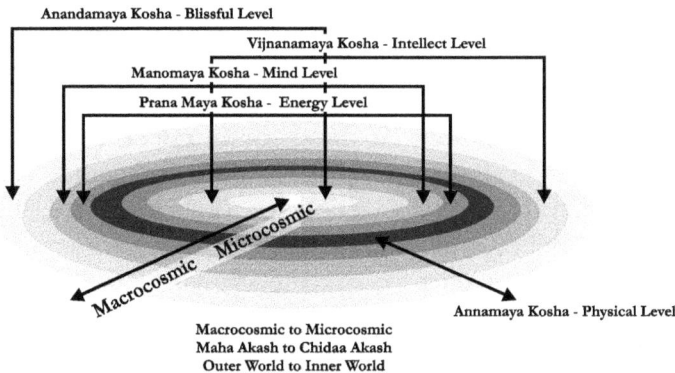

Anandamaya Kosha - Blissful Level
Vijnanamaya Kosha - Intellect Level
Manomaya Kosha - Mind Level
Prana Maya Kosha - Energy Level
Macrocosmic   Microcosmic
Annamaya Kosha - Physical Level

Macrocosmic to Microcosmic
Maha Akash to Chidaa Akash
Outer World to Inner World

fig 3:1

Yoga explains the working of any activity in a unique style. Apart from the physical body that we see and feel, there are four subtler bodies which are a part of the functioning of all our activities. They go on becoming subtler from one to the other. The first Physical is the grossest and the fifth Blissful or is the subtlest. Details of these bodies are as follows:

1. The Annamaya Kosha or the Physical or Food Body:
This body contains blood, bone, fat, skin, etc. This is the grossest level of human consciousness and is perceived through the five physical senses. The level of awareness is of the material, physical plane.

2. The Pranamaya Kosha or the Pranic Body or Vital Body:
This body is the underlying energy network of the human structure. It consists of the 'Prana' or the bio-electrical energy. It is subtler than the Annamaya Kosha. Its level of awareness is of the involuntary physiological functions. It can be seen as an 'Aura' even by naked eyes by any common person, by using certain gazing techniques. This 'Aura' can be photographed by using special cameras (Kirlian Photography Technique).

3. The Manomaya Kosha or the Mental Body:
This is subtler than the Pranic body. Its grosser level contains the Emotional Body, while the subtler level contains the psyche. Its level of awareness is of the emotional and subtler mental planes.

4. The Vijnanamaya Kosha or the Intellectual Body:
This is also called as the psychic body. It is subtle than the Manomaya kosha. It functions on the astral plane through dreams, out of body experiences and other psychic activities. Awareness is on the psychic plane.

5. The Anandamaya Kosha or the Blissful Body:
This is the subtlest Kosha. This is the transcendental

dimension of the human body. It is a balance between pleasure and pain. This is where 'bliss' is experienced, which is not an 'outcome of' or 'another name' of pleasure, but state which transcends duality.

All these five Kosha-s or bodies are overlapping in nature. Their nature is from gross to subtle, the Annamaya Kosha being the grossest and the Anandamaya Kosha being the subtlest. They share their functions to a limited level with their neighbouring Kosha-s and co-exist inside and outside our physical body.

All the principles of Prakriti are present in all these Kosha-s. The principles experienced normally, are limited to the five sense and motor principles. Though, all the other principles can be understood and experienced by any person by enhancing 'Inner Awareness', which can be developed through Yogic Practices.

Sound and Music can be experienced in all of these sheaths or bodies at different levels of consciousness, with different levels of understanding.

D. Nadi-s, Sthana-s (Registers) and Shruti-s:

1. Nadi-s : Nadi-s are energy channels in our Pranic body. They are numerous in number. Yogic texts claim them to be 72,000 in number. They extend to the mental body and also are connected to the channels of the physical body through the nervous system. fig3.2 shows the major Nadi-s in the head.

Among them 14 nadi-s are important. Sushumna, is the most important which extends from the mooladhar, root chakra, to the sahastrar, the crown chakra. Prana flows in upward direction in this nadi. Ida or Chandra nadi and Pingala or Surya nadi, positioned next to the Sushumna on the left and

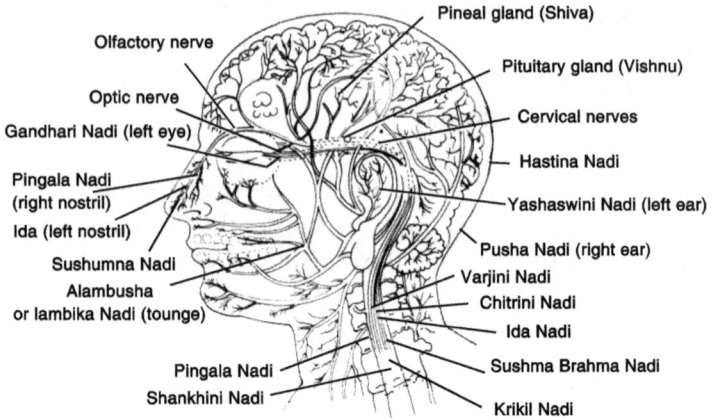

major nAdI-s in the head

fig. 3.2

right, extend till the left and right nostril, respectively. Other nadi-s are responsible for the main functions of the body.

2. Sthana: The Indian texts have used the word Sthana for registers. Sthana, in Sanskrit means the residing place. Sangeet Ratnakar has briefed about these sthana-s. The heart or Hridaya is the sthana of mandra saptaka i.e. the lower octave, throat or Kantha is the sthana of Madhya saptaka i.e. the middle octave and head or Mastaka is the sthana of tara saptaka i.e. the higher octave.

3. Shruti-s: At the heart sthana there are 22 smaller nadi-s branching from the Ida and Pingala. Air or Prana flows from these nadi-s. Due to this friction 22 microtones called as Shruti-s are sounded. **Shruti, in sanskrit means, that which can be heard.** These can be heard by well trained ears or by developing inner awareness. Similarly, by the friction sound of the Prana from 22 nadi-s each at the throat and head sthana, shruti-s can be heard. All the 3 octaves thus have 22 shruti-s each.

At every chakra, there are thousands of nadi-s branching

from the Ida and Pingala. Though, sound is generated at each nadi, majority sound frequencies cannot be perceived at the gross level of Nada, the Vaikhari nada. This is the sound level useful for performance, expression and communication with the society. So for general and social use of speech and music, we can use only 22 shruti-s. Other shruti-s and sounds are useful for self development.

E. Chakra-s:

These are the energy centres or plexuses of the Nadi-s situated in our Pranic body. They are connected to parallel nervous plexuses in our Physical body. These Chakra-s regulate the flow of Cosmic Energy to and from our Physical body, to all the other four sheaths. All these Chakra-s can receive and transmit energy simultaneously, through the subtle channels described previously as Nadi-s. Yogic texts mention about 108 Chakra-s, 7 of them being the most important. The first five, from the seven main Chakra-s, are situated close to the backbone. Fig 3.3 shows the location of the 7 main Chakra-s in the body along with the Bindu Visarga/Centre (many times termed as Chakra).

1. The Mooladhar or the Root Chakra:
This is the seat of the Vital Force, in the form known as Kundalini. This is the basic store house of energy required for our daily worldly activities. It is responsible for our survival issues and instinct. This Chakra is related to the instinct of Fear required for our survival. It is responsible for the basic energy level of a speaker/singer and his voice.

2. The Swadhishthan or the Sacral Chakra:
It is also called as the Hara. It is connected with our sexual activities and is responsible for our feelings and emotions of the past (of this life and all past lives) and all the memories. It is responsible for the arousal of desires and the crudest form of creative inspiration. It is responsible for the confidence

level of a speaker/singer and his voice.

3. The Manipur Chakra or the Solar Plexus:

It is the centre of power and activity. It is situated near the stomach. It is responsible for the enthusiasm and vigour of a speaker/singer in all aspects – learning, teaching or performing. It is responsible for digestion and assimilation of gross and subtle food i.e. intake of food and energy, even the emotional issues, including the digestion and assimilation

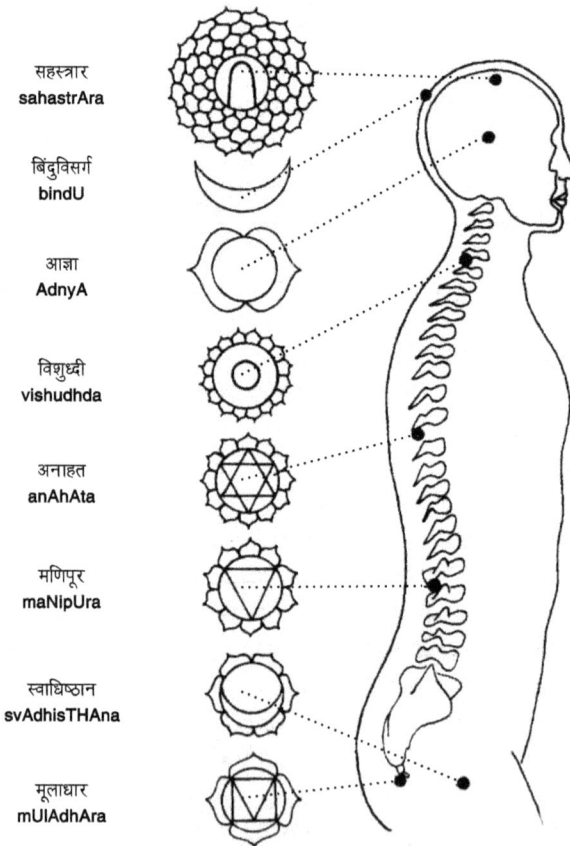

सहस्रार
sahastrAra

बिंदुविसर्ग
bindU

आज्ञा
AdnyA

विशुध्दी
vishudhda

अनाहत
anAhAta

मणिपूर
maNipUra

स्वाधिष्ठान
svAdhisTHAna

मूलाधार
mUlAdhAra

7 main chakra-s

fig 3:3

of learnt language/music and other speech/music related experiences.

4. The Anahat i.e. the Heart Chakra:

It is situated near the heart. It is the seat of present emotions and affects the speaker/singer and his voice a lot. This Chakra takes care of all the activities of the thorax including respiration. The strength of the Diaphragm, breath control and breathing (Vital) Capacity depends on the function of the Anahat Chakra. It is responsible for harmony, inspiration; regulating rhythm and time-sense, smooth movement, and emotional balancing required for speech and music. According to Yogic view sound is first manifested in the Heart Chakra, before being expressed through the Throat Chakra.

5. The Vishuddha i.e the Throat Chakra;

It is situated near the Vocal Cords. It governs the strength and movements of the activities of the larynx, pharynx, mouth and nose. These activities include swallowing, phonation and articulation, movement of the epiglottis, etc. It is the seat of expression, communication and creativity. This Chakra is responsible for linguistic skills (including its phonation and articulation skills), creative and artistic expression and creative communication, confidence of expression and communication, voice, etc. This is one of the most important Chakra-s for a speaker/singer. Any speech or musical expression and language or musical creativity, be it vocal, instrumental, prose, poetry or any creative expression is regulated by the Throat Chakra. Imbalance of this Chakra leads to stage-fear.

6. The Ajna or the Third Eye Chakra:

It is situated between the brows. It governs all the activities of the brain, eyes and ears. It is the controller of all our activities and the functions of all the Chakra-s below it. It is responsible for all the brain activities, neuro-muscular coordination, hearing, wisdom, intuitive creativity, imagination, logic, analyzing, harmony with the supreme and mastering of self activities and thoughts. It develops the higher brain functions, developing cortex activities of reasoning, thinking, invention, planning, memory and intelligence.

7. The Sahastrar i.e the Crown Chakra:
It lies just above the head. It is the main receiving centre of the Cosmic Energy. It connects our Individual Consciousness with the Cosmic Consciousness, the Individual Self with the Cosmic Self.

Ancient Indian music texts mention few other Chakra-s related to musical activities.

i. Lalana Chakra:
This Chakra also called as Talu Chakra, is situated near the soft palate. Music texts refer to its importance in vocal activities. The voice or music expressed from the Throat Chakra can become blissful only when this Lalana Chakra develops. A developed Lalana Chakra pours the Nectar of the Cosmic Bliss in the expression of a speaker/singer.

ii. Manah Chakra:
It is situated in lower forehead, a little above Ajna Chakra. This develops imagination power, visualization, etc. It is associated with the Chitta, representing the psyche, subconscious mind and memory.

iii. Soma Chakra:
This Chakra situated above Ajna, in the centre of the forehead, develops courage, humbleness, understanding of depths and details in a speech or music activity, etc.

iv. Bindu Visarga/Chakra:
This is another area often refered as Chakra that is related to Music. It is the seat of all sounds and Music in us. It is connected with the Throat Chakra. It lies between the Ajna

and Sahastrar Chakra, near the topmost tip of the brain at the back of the head. It is the seat of Wisdom. Some texts do refer it simply as 'Bindu'.

'Chakra', means 'wheel'. It is named so, as the pranic energy at these centres actually rotates spirally, forming a lotus-like structure. The rotation of every chakra, though not exact, has approximate rotation speed. This gives rise to different sounds of different frequencies. The notes thus formed are the seven musical notes. (See table 3.7 for details).These fine sounds cannot be heard by the physical ear. These sounds (along with other similar universal natural sounds) are termed as 'Anahat Nada', and can be heard by the practice of some Yogic techniques. The chord of all the seven notes sounded by the seven Chakra-s together creates the sound of 'AUM', the Cosmic Sound.

Yogi-s were aware of these sounds. So they called the physical body as 'Gatra Veena', where in Sanskrit, 'gatra' means organs and 'veena' means a lute. The concept of 'Shruti' can be understood by meditating on the music of this 'Gatra Veena'.

F. Ayurveda - The Healing Science of Yoga

Ayurveda is the healing science which explains anatomy and physiology, originating from the veda-s, parallell to yoga. Like yoga, it follows all the principles accepted by yoga, explained earlier. Ayurveda is far more than just a healing or medicinal science. Like yoga it is holistic in nature. Anatomy of Ayurveda is based on natural or dharmic laws. It is formulated initially in terms of dosha-s.

1. Three dosha-s:

Dosha-s are invisible. They are not physical by themselves but, they govern the physical process. They are the 'metabolic principles'. They are quite abstract in nature. These Dosha-s are present not only in the human body, but, are present in the universe as well. They are evident in the human body and throughout nature. These qualities are also called as guna-s. They are twenty five in number. (here the guna is used as an adjective, whereas the three Guna-s of Prakriti – Sattwa, Rajas and Tamas, are proper nouns). Dosha-s work through the five elements. The fundamental principles of these dosha-s are abstract. We should remember that the English words used for the elements, are not exact. These words are concepts having deeper, abstract, very subtle and cosmic meanings than their normal dictionary meanings.

Vata: Vata works with the space and air elements. Their functional areas are the nerve forces, sensory inputs and motion.

Pitta: Pitta functions through the element of fire and water. All motor actions including digestion and assimilation are its field of work.

Kapha: This dosha functions through the water and earth elements. The role of kapha is maintaining stability, creating friction and storing energy in latent form.

Chart showing fundamental 25 qualities (guna-s) of the three dosha-s

Vata	Pitta	Kapha
Dry	Hot	Heavy
Moving	Sharp	Cold
Cold	Light	Oily
Light	Moist	Sweet
Changable	Slightly Oily	Steady
Subtle	Fluid	Slow
Rough	Sour Smelling	Soft
Quick		Sticky
(Leads other dosha-s)		Dull
		Smooth

chart 3:2

Every person's voice can be categorized according to the following guna-s. Voice can be cultured applying the same principles lying behind balancing the dosha-s.

2. Pancha Prana:

Vata, the primary dosha is connected with prana, the life force energy. It is also called as 'vayu' in Ayurveda. It is connected with the nervous system and connects the whole body. The entire universe is a manifestation of prana. Prana is divided into five types according to its movement and direction, and its area of work. Each vayuh or prana has an assigned function and location in the body. They are:

Chart of Pancha-Prana-s or Vayuh-s

Name	Location in the Body	Function	Direction of movement	Connection with Voice	Signs of Imbalance
Prana	Brain, Head, Chest	Movement, Perception - Sensory and Intellectual, Leads other four vayuh-s	Forward and upward	Very important, Breathing Capacity, Balance of Registers and voice quality	Breathy, timid, tensed voice with varied qualities in different registers
Apana	Colon, Lower Abdomen	Elimination of wastes digestive, sexual, menstruation	Downward and outward	Expression, Communication Skills	Closed, introvert voice, non-expressive voice, without creative skills
Udana	Throat and Lungs	Speech, Memory, Movement of thoughts	Upward	Very important, speech, singing, memorizing, creating new ideas	Total or partial non-exspression, a feeling 'I have it on the tip of my tongue, but cannot say'.
Samana	Stomach, Intestines	Movements of Digestion,	Balancing	Resonance and energy in Voice, a moist effect in voice	Dry, non-resonant voice, without lower harmonics
Vyana	Heart, Whole body, Nervous System, Circulatory System, Skin	Circulation, heart rhythm	From centre to the periphery, circulating	Rhythm (laya) in speech and singing, communication with the audience and self	Non-rhythmic speech and singing, without the performance skill of 'winning the audience'

It is the udana and prana that are of special importance to a singer, though other vayu-s are also important.

chart 3:3

3. Diet:

Ayurveda decides food and its functions on the basis of its taste and divides it according to the three Guna-s. Good voice needs a balanced proportion of pitta, vata and kapha.

The diet chosen by a speaker or singer should be according to the voice quality. eg. A person with Bombaka voice should avoid food that increases vata, as vata will increase the dryness of the voice. A person with Kahula voice should avoid food which increases kapha. Simiarly, a person with dominant Narata voice should avoid pitta aggravating food. A Mishraka voice person would need to learn his voice and diet trends to decide the diet he would need to avoid.

Some charts which will help to understand the Ayurvedic diet principles are given below. Diet can be chosen, altered and decided taking into consideration a correct combination of these principles.

Chart of the six tastes

Taste	Element	Dosha	Guna
Sweet(Madhura)	Earth, water	Increases kapha, decreases pitta and vata	Sattwa
Salty(Lavan)	Water, Fire	Increases kapha and pitta, decreases vata	Rajas
Sour(Amla)	Earth, Fire	Increases pitta and kapha, deareases vata	Rajas
Pungent(Kattu)	Fire, Air	Increases vata and pitta, decreases kapha	Rajas
Bitter(Tikta)	Air, Ether (Aakash)	Increases vata, decreases pitta and kapha	Tamas
Astringent (Kashaya)	Earth, air	Increases vata, decreases pitta and kapha	Tamas

chart 3:4

4.Seasons and Tastes

The following table summarizes the tastes which are more powerful in each of the six seasons.

Seasons And Tastes

Ritu (Season)	Masa (Month)	Climate	Powerful Taste
Shishir	Magha and Phalguna (mid January to mid March)	Cold and dewy season	Bitter (Tikta)
Vasant	Chaitra and Vaishakh (mid March to mid May)	Spring season	Astringent (Kashaya)
Grishma	Jyeshtha and Aashadha (mid May to mid July)	Summer season	Pungent (Kattu)
Varsha	Shravan and Bhadrapada (mid July to mid September)	Rainy season	Sour (Amla)
Sharad	Ashvin and Kartika (mid September to mid November)	Autumn season	Salty (Lavan)
Hemant	Margshirsha and Pausha (mid November to mid January)	Winter season	Sweet (Madhura)

chart 3:5

5. Dosha-s and Daily Routine

Everyday there are two cycles of change of Vata, Pitta, or Kapha predominance. We should avoid food of the dominant dosha at the time of the dominat dosha in the cycle. The approximate times of these cycles are as follows:

First cycle:
6 a.m. to 10 a.m. – Kapha Dominance
10 a.m. to 2 p.m. – Pitta Dominance
2 p.m. to 6 p.m. - Vata Dominance

Second cycle:
6 p.m. to 10 p.m. – Kapha Dominance
10 p.m. to 2 a.m. – Pitta Dominance
2 a.m. to 6 a.m. – Vata Dominance
Similarly, dominant dosha-s in the life cycle are:
Childhood – Kapha Dominance
Young Age – Pitta Dominance
Old Age – Vata Dominance

6.Dosha-s and Voice Qualities

Followinng is a chart which shows the dosha responsible for the particular quality of Voice. Usually, for any quality two

Dosha-s and Voice Qualities

Dosha / Quality of Voice	Vata	Pitta	Kapha
Smooth Register Shifting	1	2	3
Sweetness	2	1	1
Energy	3	2	1
Intensity	3	2	1
Flexibility	1	3	2
Good Hearing Capacity	1	2	3
Broadmindedness	1	2	3
Ability of Quick tempo	1	2	3
Coordination	1	2	-
Creativity	Force, Movement	Expression, action	Content
Communication	1	2	3
Breath Control	3	2	1
Breathing Capacity	3	2	1
Vocal range	1	2	3
Ability of Modulation	1	2	3
Muscle Tone	3	2	1
Muscle Strength	3	2	1
Melody	Tempo, flow	coordination	Consistency, smoothness
Harmony	2	1	3
Texture	3	2	1
Rhythm Understanding	1	2	3
Taala (Complex rhythm patterns)	3	1	2
Planning	2	1	3

chart 3:6

77

dosha-s are dominant, sometimes all three. Its importance is depicted with numbers, where 1 is more important than 2. This list is not exhaustive.

G. Nada Yoga

The word Nada comes from the Sanskrit root 'nada' which means to flow, vibrate, and pulsate. The etymological or the root meaning of Nada is a process or a stream of consciousness. Though normally, the word Nada means sound, the Yogic view of 'Nada' includes the whole universe in the vibratory form.

Nada is classified in different ways. The methods relevant to our topic are given below:

1. Ahat and Anahat:

The sound formed by friction is 'Ahat' and the sound that has always existed in the universe and is formed without any friction is called as 'anahat' sound. This is just a rough definition (there is friction in 'anahat' sound also, but on a very subtle level, which cannot be perceived by our five physical senses). Yoga is the art and science of understanding the anahat nada. But, this music can be perceived only by self. Its joy and happiness cannot be shared with others. The music of Ahat nada on the other hand can be shared with people around us. Hence, the art of music as an aesthetic form of creation and understanding of 'Ahat' nada was developed. Sharangadeva in Sangeeta Ratnakar elaborates this point.

ध्यानमेकाग्रचित्तैकसाध्यं न सुकरं नृणाम् ||
तस्मादत्र सुखोपायं श्रीमन्नादमनाहतम् || १.२.१६५ ||
dhyaanamekaagrachittaikasaadhyam na sukaram nRNAm ||
tasmaadatra sukhopaayam shrImannaadamanaahatam
|| 1.2.165 ||

meaning: meditation (of anahat nada) is a means for concentration of the mind and is not suitable for enjoyment in general.

Hence, Ahat nada should be used as a means for happiness.

गुरूपदिष्टमार्गेण मुनयः समुपासते ||
सोऽपि रक्तिविहीनत्वान्न मनोरंजको नृणाम् || १.२.१६६ ||

gurupadiShTamaargeNa munayah samupaasate ||
so-pi raktivihInatvaanna manoranjako nRNaam
|| 1.2.166 ||

meaning: training of anahat nada is given to yogi-s
by their guru-s (masters).
But, as it does not have the potential to attract others,
it cannot be enjoyable to people(in general).

तस्मादाहतनादस्य श्रुत्यादिद्वारतो ऽखिलम् ||
गेयं वितन्वतो लोकरंजनं भवभंजनम् || १.२.१६७ ||

tasmaadaahatanaadasya shrutyaadidvaarato – khilam 11
geyam vitanvato lokaranjanam bhavabhanjanam
|| 1.2.167 ||

meaning: Hence, I will elaborate on shruti and other facts
about Ahat nada which can be entertaining to people as well as
they can get rid of all the worldly sorrows by it.

2. Nada and Dhwani:
Though in Yogic reference Nada means any vibration, the meaning of nada is limited to musical ahat sound in Music. Dhwani means any musical or non-musical sound.

3. Musical and Non-musical:
According to physics of sound the meaning of musical sound is that, it has a regular and repeated wave pattern of vibrations and non-musical sound, also termed as noise has an irregular wave pattern of vibrations.

4. Vaikhari, Madhyama, Pashyanti and Para:
Sound occurs in four levels and dimensions. These four levels of sound relate to frequency, fineness, perceiving level and strength as follows:

i. Vaikhari – The coarse (ordinary, audible, material) sound. It is this level of Nada that is used in speaking or singing.

ii. Madhyama – The mental sound. With even little practice of Music or Yoga, a common man can hear, understand and feel this level of Nada. To understand the concept of shruti, we should practice inner awareness to reach this level.

iii. Pashyanti – The visualized sound

iv. Para – The transcendent sound.

Pashyanti and Para being very subtle levels of Nada are very difficult to understand and explain. It is however possible to perceive and experience these Nada-s by practicing Nada Yoga Sadhana, meditation, or even by developing inner awareness in singing.

Nada Yoga is Yoga of Sounds. It is the path of experiencing the quality of sounds, both 'Ahat' and 'Anahat', and the way they affect people. We have sounds that are coarse and sounds that are fine. The finest sounds can be heard by practicing 'Inner Awareness'. In Yoga we call them the inner sounds – 'Antarnada'.

Indian culture including its Music has its origin in Nada Yoga, the awareness of 'Unheard', 'Anahat' sounds. Yogi-s who were musicians too, experienced the similarities and harmony of the sounds of the Chakra-s and the Audible and Inaudible Sounds of Nature. This was the basis of derivation of the Musical Scale. Different nada-s or tones relate and affect our different Chakra-s or the psychic centres.

Nada Yoga, the meditation of the inner sounds, helps us to reach deeper states of consciousness and has a strong liberating effect in dissolving the deepest blocks and inhibitions of the mind.

In his Treatise 'Yoga-Taravali', Adi Shankaracharya says, "By one who is desirous of attaining perfection in Yoga, Nada alone has got to be closely heard (meditated upon) with a calm mind, having abandoned all thoughts."

सदाशिवोक्तानि सपादलयावधानानि वसंति लोके |
नादानुसंधानसमाधिमेकम् मन्यामहे मान्यतमं लयानाम् | |

sadaashivoktaani sapaadalayaavadhaanaani vasanti loke l
nadaanusandhanasamaadhimekam manyaamahe maanyatam
layaanaam l l

meaning: Lord Sadashiva (Shankara) has said that there are one lac
twentyfive thousand ways of attaining 'chitta-laya' (realization). Among
them I believe nadanusandhana (becoming merged with inner sound) to
be the best commendable way.

The Nada Bindu Upanishad, Taitariya Upanishad, Hatha Yoga and many more treatises have stated the importance of Nada in Yoga practice. These treatises have proposed the practice of Nada Yoga as it accelerates the process of the expanding of Consciousness and Awareness.

For a Nada-Yogi it is important to be aware of the sounds, which are found in the dimensions, other than physical - the mental and psychic. He has to go on unfolding the layers of 'Nada', from Vaikhari to Para. Consciousness gets expanded to deeper levels while practicing Nada Yoga.

H: The Universe and Nada or Nadabrahma

In the word Nadabrahma, Brahma means Supreme Reality. So Nadabrahma means sound of the Supreme Reality, the Universe or the Cosmos.

A Nada-Yogi experiences the macrocosmic universe as a projection of sound vibrations and experiences the concept that the whole world has developed from sound alone.

The principle behind concept of Nadabrahma is that, the

Universe has unfolded from the eternal sound of OM. That means that the material, the mental, the psychic and the intellectual universe have all originated from Nada-Brahma, the sound universe. It is the way the Nada-Yogi experiences 'Reality'. It manifests itself in the form of vibrations, of which the finest vibrations, the Para Nada, vibrate at such a high frequency that it lies far beyond the range of normal human senses and understanding. Some texts mention the word 'Apara Nada', which means devoid of vibrations, a state beyond vibrations.

The Upanishad-s (particularly the Nada-Bindu-Upanishad and the Hansa-Upanishad) and the Vedas describe that in the beginning there was 'Nothing'. This 'Nothingness' of the universe existed as sound. The sound was unending; the sound was the only existing 'Reality'. The universe evolved from sound, and therefore the fundamental structure of the universe is based on Nada or sound vibrations.

I: The Centre of Nada in the Body

Nada-Yogi-s locate the sound centre in Bindu. Bindu is the spark of energy which has the potential to create and transform. This energy is in the form of Nada. There are eight Bindu-s at the centre of every Chakra – the seven main and the Bindu Visarga. The lowermost called as 'Adhah Bindu' in the Mooladhar, in the Kundalini, and the uppermost called as 'Para Bindu', in the Sahastrar. The Bindu Visarga which is located at the top of the back of the head is the seat of Nada in the body. It is therefore the centre for music, too. Through music, the mind can be tuned to the finest vibrations and thereby prepared for the transcendent Nada.

J: Relation of Yoga, Voice and Music

If we understand the roots of the Art of Speech and Music, the path towards the ultimate purpose of human life becomes clear. Music and/or a musical voice have also the potential to become the path and the goal, together.

1. Metaphysical Importance:

Sharangadev in his text Sangeet Ratnakar (13th century A.D.) has elaborated on the metaphysical aspects of voice and music. He explains how any sound is produced from subtlest to subtle, and from subtle to gross, i.e. from Para to Vaikhari. He has also explained the importance of Chakra-s in music. He has emphasized the necessity of knowledge and understanding of the depths and the non-technical and non-material view of music as a whole and its relative terms like Shruti, Grama, Moorchhana, etc.

Like Sharangadeo, many renowned musicians of the ancient times have emphasized on the metaphysical aspect of music and its importance in learning music. Bharata in this treatise NatyaShashtra, Pandit Ahobal in his treatise Sangeet Parijat, Sangeetacharya Ramavtaar Veer in his book Bharatiya Sangeet ka Itihaas, Pandit Vasant Madhav Khadilkar in his book Gandharva Veda are few examples among those who have also emphasized on knowing these metaphysical concepts. These great musicians were regular practitioners of Yoga, and had a deep knowledge of many other sciences like Ayurveda, Sphotavada, Astronomy, Mathematics, etc. Their view to music was a holistic one. They emphasized that any musician or performer should have a thorough insight of 'all' the aspects of Music - the practical, theoretical and metaphysical, all together.

2. Role of Emotions and Mind:

Emotions and character play a vital role in voice production and singing. We have seen in Chapter 2, fig.2.4 that sensory branches of the Vagus Nerve signal the feelings i.e. emotions to and from the brain. These signals control the movements of the voice. They send signals to all the articulators and the larynx, which affect the pitch, intensity, timbre and the tempo of the voice. Depression and sorrow lowers the soft palate which makes the sound nasal. Suppression of emotions results into a soft and low tone. A habitually tensed person produces a higher pitch level than a relaxed person. Sharp and nasal voice shows a nagging personality. A harsh voice is produced by person habituated to anger. A fearful or timid person has a shaky or a very feeble voice. A mentally unstable person speaks very fast. A lethargic person is a very slow speaker.

The Emotional body lies next to the Pranic body. Hence they influence each other to a large extent. Similarly, the Pranic body lies next to the Physical body, influencing it to a large extent. Emotional fluctuations influence the Pranic body which further change the physical characters, affecting immediately and largely on the voice. Emotions are a part of the Mental body or the mind. So fluctuations in the thinking pattern of the mind also affect the voice in a similar way.

Usually, one who can speak should be able to sing. But, practically we do not observe this happening around us. This is because of improper hearing or an incapability of good hearing i.e. differentiating between sounds, their qualities, their frequencies, etc. The physiological mechanism of 'voice' is controlled by the psychological part of 'will'. If this 'will' does not function properly then there is no mechanical aid or method to make one sing. If this 'will' is present or created, any speaking voice can be trained and cultured to sing.

From the table showing the left and right brain functions in Chapter II, we can see that during expression, voice production or singing, a coordination of the left and right brain is necessary. A coordination of knowledge and creativity, art and science, body and mind, heart and head, emotions and intellect, rhythm and tempo, pitch and scale, etc. is necessary for any speaker/singer at any and every stage.

Yoga, which means to join, can be one of the best coordinators for all these speaking or singing activities. For a holistic approach the gross has to join hands with the subtle.

K: Metaphysics of Production of Voice

The production of sound as described by these ancient music texts can be summarized as follows: First in the subtlest part of our body a desire is produced to produce a sound (in the brain). This gives inspiration to the mind. The mind stimulates the 'Agni' (fire element). The 'Agni' i.e the fire, pushes and stimulates the 'Vayu' i.e the air element. This Vayu travels from the Brahma Granthi (a knot in the Kundalini, at the Mooladhar) upwards crossing the paths of the Chakra-s. The subtlest form of sound is produced at the Brahma Granthi. This sound travels upwards from the path of navel, heart, throat and head, then again travels downwards and is produced as 'Voice' from the mouth. The subtlest sound becomes grosser and grosser in this process, till it reaches the mouth where it becomes so gross that it can be heard by the normal human ear. This path of sound is from 'Para' to 'Vaikhari' through 'Pashyanti' and 'Madhyama'. It is explained in Sangeeta Ratnakar by Sharangadeva as:

आत्मा विवक्षमाणोऽयं मनः प्रेरयते मनः ||
देहस्थं वन्हिमाहन्ति स प्रेरयति मारूतम् || १.३.३ ||

aatmaa vivakshamaaNo-yam manah prerayate manah
dehastham vanhimaahanti sa prerayati maarutam || 1.3.3 ||1

meaning: when the self (soul) desires to speak, it gives inspiration to the mind. Then the mind strikes the fire in the body. This further stimulates the air element (vital force).

ब्रह्मग्रन्थिस्थितः सोऽथ क्रमादूर्ध्वपथे चरन् ||
नाभिहृत्कण्ठमूर्धास्येष्वाविर्भावयति ध्वनिम् || १.३.४ ||

brahmagranthishitah so-tha kramaadUrdhvapathe charan 11
naabhihRtkaNTHamUrdhaasyeSHvaavirbhaavayati dhvanim 1
1 1.3.4 1 1

meaning: the air (vayu) which dwells in the brahmagranthi
(a knot near the anal region) then rises up from
navel, heart, throat, head and mouth and manifests as sound.

नकारं प्राणनामानं दकारमनलं विदुः ||
जातः प्राणाग्निसंयोगात्तेन नादोऽभिधीयते || १.३.६ ||
nakaaram praaNanaamaanam dakaaramanalam viduh 11
jaatah praaNagnisanyogaattena naado-bhidhIyate 11 1.3.6 11

meaning: Scholars know that nakara (the sound of 'n') is the name of the
air (prana) and dakaara (the sound of 'd') is the fire. As air and fire
combine to form sound it is called as nada.

L: How Yogic Practices help Speakers / Singers

The traditional way of culturing the voice and developing
musical ability is by learning from a teacher or in an institution.
It is a process of several years.

Today, the life style has changed. Heavy cultural exchanges are
changing the basic thinking patterns of people. The
technological changes are creating an imbalance in mental,
emotional and physical behavior of people. Today's world is
facing new and severe problems of speed, technology,
commercialization, audio, visual and press media, heavy
changes of speech techniques and musics of the world. It has
become extremely difficult for a speaker/singer to balance the
learning, teaching and performing speed. To cope up with these
new problems, new teaching methods have to be developed.

'Yoga' is a solution to all these problems together, as it works
on the body and the mind together. By the practice of 'Yoga',
any artist becomes physically, emotionally and mentally stable
and healthy to face all the above mentioned problems and keep
pace with the time.

For learning, teaching and performing, good health, good
neuro-muscular coordination and breath control are necessary.

As Yoga works on the body, breath and mind together, training, learning and understanding of language and music becomes easier, deeper and faster. A task which could otherwise need several years can be achieved within few years, by regular practice of Yoga.

Yoga is a blessing to mankind. Yoga is the union of the 'Jeevatma' with the 'Paramatma' i.e. the Individual Consciousness with the Cosmic Consciousness. Though Yogic Practices have been developed basically for spiritual evolution, they are equally beneficial to every individual, in every walk of life, be it science or any form of art, including theatre and literature. Music is no exception.

The purpose and origin of word, language and music seen in all cultures is similar. Language was developed for expression and communication. Music was developed to praise the Lord or for spiritual evolution. In India, music was developed by Yogi-s i.e. sages. The basic principles and effects of Music and Yoga are universal.

Yogi-s were aware that music soothes the mind. They were aware that when speech was linked with a musical voice it was more effective. Music was developed as a Yogic Practice in particular and also as complimentary to many other Yogic Practices. Yoga is the melody and harmony of the unseen inner self and music is the melody and harmony of the seen outer self. So, both can harmonize our inner and outer self together.

Yogic Practices effectively work on all the levels viz. physical, emotional, mental, intellectual and spiritual, individually and collectively. Yogic Practices also develop the inner good qualities of the character of our being, making us socially healthy and ethical. These social and individual ethics are not followed as a burden or out of compulsion. They are an overflow of our stress-free and contented inner being. Yogic Practices make us contented, successful, ethical, energetic, stress-free and healthy individuals, with an enchanting personality.

Yogi-s have experienced that the Cosmic Life Energy is received through the energy plexuses called Chakra-s (explained earlier). These Chakra-s transmit the received energy, to the physical body, through the subtle Nadi-s.

Regular physical exercises practiced by a musician, (including those taught as part of music lessons and practice) do not bear the subtle quality of activating the Chakra-s and receiving extra Cosmic energy. To activate the latent potentials of our being these normal exercises are not enough.

On the other hand, the Yogic Postures and other Yogic practices activate the energy plexuses i.e. Chakra-s, to receive extra energy. This quality of Yoga makes it different from all other forms of exercises. It is only because of these subtle qualities of Yoga that the latent musical potential is stimulated, developing the musical ability of a musician, within unbelievably short span of time.

Now, we shall see few of the important aspects of Yoga which are directly beneficial for voice production. We shall see how Kriya-s, Asana-s, Bandha-s, Mudra-s, Pranayam and Omkar help. All these practices help to expand the 'Awareness' step by step, from Physical to Spiritual level. Though every practice of Yoga works holistically on all the Kosha-s, each practice emphasizes and concentrates specially on certain kosha-s.
* Asana-s and Kriya-s are meant for the health and balancing of Annamaya Kosha
* Pranayam for Pranamaya Kosha
* Mudra-s and Bandha-s for the Pranamaya and Manomaya Kosha together
* Dharana and Dhyana for Manomaya Kosha
* Sankalpa for Vidhyanamaya Kosha
* Prayer for Anandamaya Kosha

· Omkar for all the Kosha-s together.

The practice of Dharana (concentration) and Dhyana (meditation) help a speaker/singer in many ways. The mind becomes balanced and calm. There is a positive change in personality and character. This helps in making the voice more confident and smooth, steady and rich in texture.

Here is a list of some kriya-s, yogasana-s, mudra-s, bandha-s and pranayam-s beneficial especially for a speaker/singer. I have mentioned their techniques in short. The benefits mentioned here are related to voice, voice production, singing and voice related. Their detailed technique and general benefits can be found in many texts on Yoga.

Any Yogic Practice should be learnt under a good and authorized teacher. **Also the do's and don'ts should be followed strictly, otherwise it may lead to negative results.** Yoga should never be practiced with a competitive spirit. It should be chosen and practiced as per our constitution and requirements. The Yoga techniques mentioned here are effective and easy. This is not an exhaustive list. There are many schools and styles of practicing Yoga.

An important factor to be followed in any Yoga practice is 'Awareness'. We should remember that without awareness any Yoga Practice gives limited results. The deeper the awareness, faster and better will be the results.

It is important to remember that Yoga should be learnt under proper guidance.

Some important rules to be followed for healthy and fruitful Yoga practice are:

· Always start and end every Yoga Practice with Deha Dharana and Prana Dharana i.e. with closed eyes be aware of all the happenings and changes in the body and breath, respectively. We have to understand the rule that **'energy follows awareness'**.

- Practice Yoga with closed eyes and with full Inner Awareness, unless specified otherwise.
- Pay more attention to quality than the quantity. In the race of gaining quantity never give the cost of quality.
- One should practice Yoga paying due respect to self capacity.
- Never exceed self capacity, at the same time stretch the body and mind to such an extent as to feel comfortable and relaxed after releasing the stretch. **Never stretch yourself to the level of 'pain'.**
- Always breathe through the nose and breathe normally throughout the practice, unless mentioned otherwise.
- Yoga Kriya-s, Yogasana-s, Mudra-s, Bandha-s and Pranayama-s should always be practiced on an empty stomach.
- After any yoga practice one should always feel fresh and happy. If you lack these feelings please check whether the practice is done with proper precautions and that the practice does not exceed your capacity.
- Daily and scheduled practice is necessary to bring about the changes beyond the physical level.

1. Yoga Kriya-s:

Also called as 'Shuddhi Kriya-s', they are the cleansing processes or agents. They help us to get rid of impurities, toxins and blocks in the physical, pranic, emotional and mental bodies.

i. Trataka

It is a simple but powerful 'Kriya'. First we gaze at an object with open eyes and then, with closed eyes try to visualize the picture in the eyebrow centre. These two phases are called as Bahir Trataka and Antar Trataka, respectively. It cleanses the

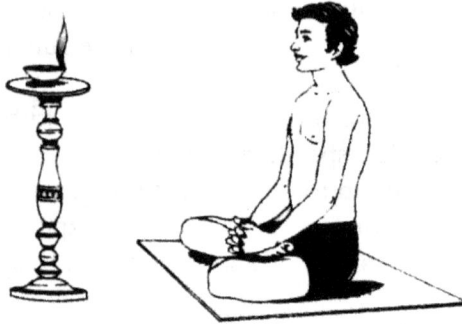

fig 3:4

nadi-s of the brain. The Third Eye Chakra is stimulated. Trataka develops the higher brain functions, developing cortex activities of reasoning, thinking, invention, planning, memory and intelligence. This leads to better sound and musical perception and voice production.

ii. Kapalbhati

In this Kriya we have to do forceful, fast and jerky active exhalations using the abdominal muscles and the inhalation is passive. This cleanses the full respiratory and voice tract and is stimulating to the brain cells. It cleans the sinuses. It stimulates the nerves of the larynx, pharynx and the brain. Thus helping better breathing capacity, good resonation, better memory and good synchronization needed for voice production and singing. It activates the Mooladhar and Swadhishthan Chakra-s. This helps to improve the energy level in the voice and builds confidence. It improves the depth in the voice and it cleanses the abdominal resonators.

iii. Agnisar

Apply Udiyan Bandha and flap the abdominal muscles fast. This process is called Agnisar Kriya. It helps in cleansing and stimulating the abdomen. It cleanses the abdominal resonators, helping the development of lower harmonics in the voice, developing depth in the voice. It strengthens the abdominal muscles and diaphragm, helping good control of the breath and voice. It also activates the 'Swadhishthan' and 'Manipur Chakra', helping to develop enthusiasm necessary for learning, performing and teaching.

iv. Dhauti:
a. Jivhamooladhauti
The root of the tongue is given a light massage by the first and second finger and then twisted. This helps to make the tongue flexible and the tongue root strong, helping in good articulation.

b. Kapalarandhradhauti
With the help of the thumb, the area between the soft and hard palate is given a light massage. This rejuvenates the inner walls of the mouth making them softer for better articulation. It stimulates the nadi-s and nerve endings near the soft and hard palate. This kriya also helps to keep the nasal and head sinuses clean for good resonation and sweeter voice.

c. Karnarandhradhauti
The tip of the first fingers of both the hands is used to massage the entrance of the outer ear canal. This keeps the outer ear clean. It stimulates the middle and inner ear. This helps to enhance our hearing capacity.

d. Vesan Dhauti
The two ends of a rubber catheter are inserted in each nostril simultaneously and pulled out from the throat. The catheter is then joined and moved in such a way, that the two ends come out of the nose. The catheter is rubbed to give a gentle massage to the upper tip of the nasopharynx. This stimulates and cleanses the nasopharynx and the head sinuses making them more sensitive to vibrations. This helps in better resonation. The brain cells are also stimulated.

e. Jala Dhauti
Drink 3-4 litres of luke warm, water with some salt, at a

stretch, without pause. Then, give a light press with the 2 middle fingers to the root of the tongue. All the drunken water will be vomited out, along with extra mucus, extra pitta, and toxins from the stomach, esophagus and larynx. This also stimulates these organs. This helps in developing the heart functions.

f. Danda Dhauti

Drink 2-3 litres of luke warm water, with some salt, at a stretch, without pause. Gulp one end of a special rubber pipe catheter used for Danda Dhauti. With care, allow the gulped end of the pipe to reach the stomach. Then give a soft upward jerk to the abdominal muscles by doing Udiyan Bandha. Immediately, all the drunken water will start flowing out of the pipe because of the siphen action along with the water. This will expel extra mucus, extra pitta, and toxins from the stomach, esophagus and larynx, this kriya also stimulates all these organs. The health of the heart is improved, thus improving the laya, rhythm understanding.

iv. Neti:

Neti helps to get rid of sinus disorders and nasal allergies.

a. Jalaneti

Using a specially designed pot with a nozzle, the nostrils are cleaned with lukewarm water one by one, with a special

<u>fig 3:5</u>

technique. Jalaneti is refreshing and the nose becomes pleasantly open. The entire nasopharynx is relaxed and cleaned from inside. Mucus, dust and dirt, even pollen and allergy provoking particles are gently rinsed out. As the head sinuses have their openings in the nasopharynx, they are also cleaned and stimulated.

b. Sutraneti
A rubber catheter is inserted in each nostril (one at a time) and pulled out from the throat. The catheter is rubbed to give a

fig 3:6

gentle massage to the nasopharynx. This stimulates and cleanses the nasopharynx and the head sinuses making them more sensitive to vibrations. This helps in better resonation.

2.Yogasana-s:

These are physical postures that help to enhance physical and mental health, keeping the body and the mind in a state to render a performance happily. The joints become flexible building up the muscle tone and strength. This helps in attaining a good posture and sustaining it for long hours.

There are many asana-s, but, I have mentioned below few of them which help in voice production. They strengthen the functions of lungs, diaphragm, throat and brain and the breathing capacity. They make these organs flexible. This helps better blood circulation for those organs. This helps the coordination of brain, lungs, throat and mouth activities required for speech and singing. We shall see few Yogasana-s and their benefits regarding the speakers'/singers' musical ability and development of the voice.

i. Sarvangasan:
Called as the shoulder stand, here lying on the back, the legs and the trunk are lifted up. They are kept in a straight line by

सर्वांगासन

fig 3:7

supporting the trunk on the shoulders. The throat and the brain get ample blood supply. This asana helps in strengthening the laryngeal muscles, in developing memory and creativity. It develops the functions of the brain. On a deeper level, it activates the Vishuddha Chakra, because of the chin lock.

ii. Pawanmuktasan for Joints:
These are wind releasing techniques used for all the joints. Different Yoga schools follow different variations, all being equally effective. Pawanamuktasan helps to release toxins from joints and makes them flexible and healthy. It helps in developing a steady posture and balancing the flow of 'Prana'. It also helps in general health and coordination necessary for learning and performing.

iii. Matsyasan:

Lying down on the back, the legs are folded in Padmasan. With the help of the hands the top of the head is rested on the ground. This posture helps in building good breathing capacity, strengthens the intercostal muscles and lungs. It helps in developing memory. It activates the Vishuddha Chakra.

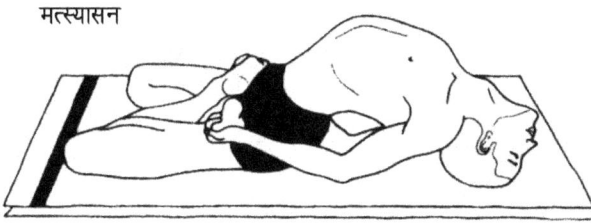

मत्स्यासन

fig 3:8

iv. Bhujangasan:

It is called as the serpent posture. Lying down on the stomach, the head is lifted with the help of the pressure on the palms. This gives a backward bend to the upper backbone. It gives a stretch to the chest. It helps in developing breathing capacity and helps in developing correct posture of the spine. It strengthens the thoracic and the laryngeal muscles.

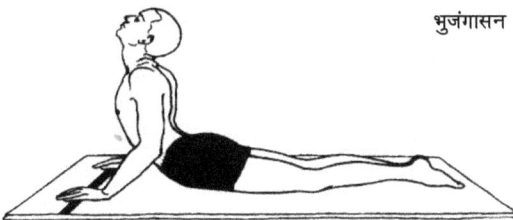

भुजंगासन

fig 3:9

v. Padmasan

Padmasan or the lotus posture is a meditative posture. This is a special cross-legged posture with the left/right heel on the right/left thigh and the right/left heel on the left/right thigh, respectively. This asana helps to develop steadiness, develops physical and mental stability and calms the mind.

पद्मासन

<u>fig 3:10</u>

vi. Parvatasan

Sitting in a Padmasan, we have to join the palms and lift them above the head, such that the shoulders touch the ears. This asana helps in developing the breathing capacity, i.e. the lung capacity. It helps in activating the dormant air sacs. It also strengthens the thoracic muscles. As a variation it can be practiced with any comfortable sitting posture with an erect spine.

पर्वतासन

<u>fig 3:11</u>

vii. Shavasan

In this Asana we have to lie down in a comfortable position with closed eyes. This is a relaxing posture. It helps in strengthening the mind and develops creativity. It helps in releasing physical and mental stresses, thus helping good circulation of blood and nerve impulses. The panch prana-s are balanced. This helps to develop a good voice and good expression. It also helps in balancing the flow of 'Prana'. This asana should be done as a daily practice. It is one of the best relaxation techniques.

शवासन

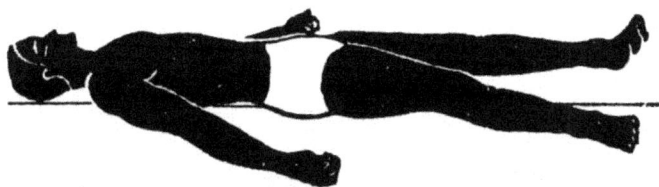

fig 3:12

3.Mudra-s

Mudra-s are of two types: Asana Mudra-s and Hasta (hand) Mudra-s. Both of them directly act upon the endocrine system. The secretion of hormones is regulated. Our personality grows positively. Mudra-s regulate the flow of Prana in our body and mind. As a good personality is needed to be a good speaker/singer, all the mudra-s will be helpful in one way or the other. Mudra-s mentioned below are especially helpful for speaker/singers. They strengthen the thyroid, parathyroid, pituitary and pineal glands and activate and balance the Chakra-s and the electro-magnetic circulation.

i. Yoga Mudra:

Sitting in Vajrasan or Padmasan, the head is made to touch the ground. This helps in digestion and maintaining physical and mental stability. It also enhances concentration and memory. As the lower abdomen is pressed a lot, it activates the 'Mooladhar', 'Swadhisthan' and 'Manipur' Chakra-s. This enhances the Udana Vayu and fire movement in upward direction enhancing

<u>fig 3:13</u>

memory and all brain functions.

ii. Sinha Mudra (Lion Symbol):

This mudra has many variations, all giving similar benefits. In a sitting or standing posture the tongue is pulled out of the mouth and the chin is locked. Along with it the mouth is stretched as much as possible. In one variation a roaring sound

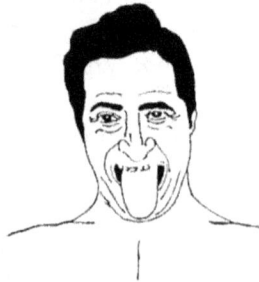

<u>fig 3:14</u>

is also made with the posture. This mudra makes the articulators flexible, i.e. the tongue, cheeks, lips, soft and hard palate and gums. It also strengthens the larynx. This helps in making the voice sweet. As it activates the cranial nerves, it enhances general health and neuro-muscular coordination. It activates the 'Vishuddha' and the 'Swadhishthan' Chakra-s. It removes the emotional stresses and blocks in the passage of expression, making the voice stress-free, energetic and bringing clarity to it.

iii. Brahma Mudra:

It is series of four positions of the neck, done with total inner awareness. Its benefits accelerate as the awareness goes deeper and deeper. This Mudra strengthens the larynx. It activates all the cranial nerves enhancing general health, health of the brain and neuro-muscular coordination. It activates the 'Vishuddha'

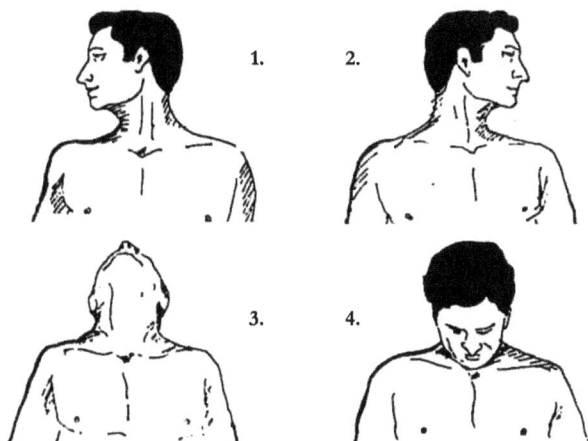

fig 3:15

Chakra. It develops memory.

iv. Ashwini Mudra:

In this mudra the muscles at the anal region are contracted and released alternatively. This Mudra helps in activating and regulating the Mooladhar Chakra. It gives strength and energy to the voice and helps flexibility of its Intensity, enhancing the intensity range.

v. Jnana Mudra:

This is a hand mudra. The tip of the thumb and the first finger are joined and the other three fingers kept open together. This Mudra activates the brain cells and develops intellect, wisdom and creativity. It also develops memory and removes mental

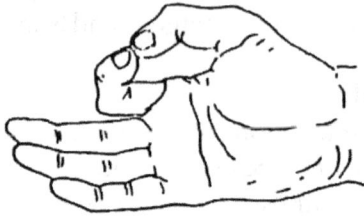

fig 3:16

stresses, making the mind calm and quiet.

vi. Prana Mudra:

The tips of the thumb, little finger and the third finger are joined and the first two fingers kept open together. This Mudra regulates the Prana. This helps in developing good stamina, good control over the voice and breath. It also builds up the lung capacity i.e. the breathing capacity.

fig 3:17

vii. Linga Mudra:

In this hand mudra, fingers of both the hands are interlocked and one thumb kept open. This helps to generate heat in the body. As a speaker/singer needs a higher than the normal temperature level in the larynx, this mudra helps in maintaining the required body temperature especially in air conditioned rooms or in cool weather. This Mudra also helps in curing colds

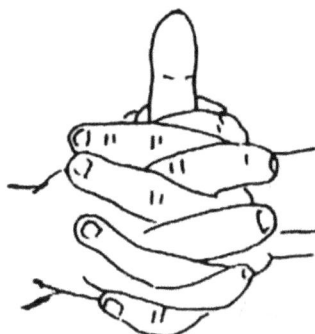

fig 3:18

and coughs.

4.Bandha-s

Bandha-s are postures used to lock the flow of Prana at certain areas in the body. They are usually practiced along with Mudra-s and Pranayam-s. These Bandha-s help to accelerate the benefits of the respective Mudra-s and Pranayam-s.

i. Jivha Bandha or the Tongue Lock

The tongue is rolled backward and its tip is made to touch the soft palate. This Bandha strengthens the tongue, its root and the upper larynx. It regulates the flow of Prana in the head region just above the hard and soft palate. It develops the Lalana Chakra bringing a blissful tone to the voice.

fig 3:19

ii. Jalandhar Bandha or the Chin Lock

The chin is pressed on the chest. Either positive or negative pressure is built at the throat region. It is helpful in any musical activity and ability, as it energizes the Throat Chakra. It regulates the flow of Prana in the throat and mouth region and the upper

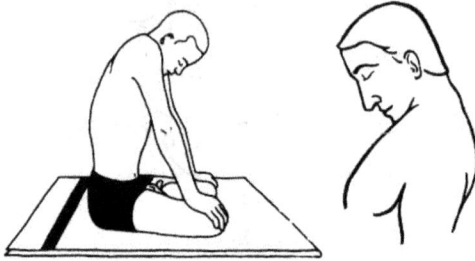

fig 3:20

chest region.

iii. Udiyan Bandha or the Diaphragm Lock

The abdominal muscles are contracted upwards, locking the Prana at the diaphragm. It helps in strengthening the diaphragm and the abdominal muscles. This helps control of the breath and develops steadiness in the voice. It also helps to bring depth to the voice, i.e. develops lower harmonic resonance. It activates the Manipur Chakra, helping to develop the required enthusiasm for a speaker/singer and his voice.

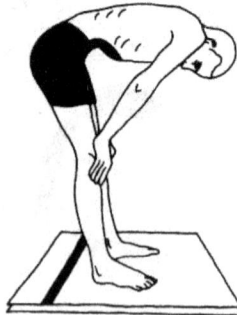

fig 3:21

iv. Moola Bandha (Contraction of the Anal Region)

In this Bandha, the anal muscles are contracted, not allowing the flow of Prana to be released, developing a pressure in the anal region. This Bandha helps in activating the Mooladhar Chakra. It strengthens the voice adding energy to it. It also develops a control over the intensity of the voice.

5. Pranayam:

Before understanding Pranayam first let us understand the meaning of 'Prana'. Prana is the life force energy present in all our five Kosha-s. It works subtle in the Mental, Intellectual and Blissful Bodies, but, actively in the Pranic and Physical body.

The word Pranayam is made of two words – 'Prana' and 'Ayam'. *Prana* means the life force energy and *Ayam* means the regulation or balancing. So Pranayam means the balancing and regulation of Prana. It is done with the help of 'Breath' as breath is that form of Prana which can be handled and understood with ease.

Pranayam-s are special breathing techniques developed by Yogi-s to increase and balance the Pranic flow. Though superficially they resemble general breathing exercises which are meant to keep the physical body healthy, Pranayam-s are specially developed to balance the Prana level (life force energy) of all the five Kosha-s, specially the Pranic and Manomaya Kosha, using breath as its vehicle. Pranayam-s are also practiced along with Kumbhaka i.e. the holding of breath.

In Yogic practice also, all the four breathing techniques mentioned in Chapter 1 are practiced. But, when we practice them as Yoga Shvasan (meaning yogic breathing), then differences like 'Inner Awareness', Deha Dharana and Prana Dharana, make these breathing patterns change their level of depth from physical to holistic, bringing about faster and deeper changes.

In general all Pranayam-s help in increasing the breathing capacity and in balancing the body and mind. Practicing Pranayam regularly strengthens the diaphragm and lungs. If practiced along with Bandha-s and Kumbhaka, the breath holding capacity increases. So, the capacity to sustain a note or melody increases. Now let us discuss the Pranayam-s which are important for voice-culture.

i. Bhastrika Pranayam:

We have to inhale and exhale rapidly and heavily. It cures disorders of the respiratory system. It removes congestion in lungs and nasal tract, apart from increasing the breathing potential.

ii. Ujjayi Pranayam:

In this Pranayam we have to contract the throat area and during exhalation force the air in the lungs with a friction in the throat. It strengthens the pharyngeal and laryngeal muscles. On a deeper level, it enhances the qualities of the Throat and Ajna Chakra-s.

iii. Bhramari Pranayam:

In this Pranayam a high frequency humming sound like a honey bee is made during exhalation. Through Bhramari we become sensitive to finer vibrations and become one with the sound vibrations. During Bhramari our whole head and the entire body is filled with fine sound vibrations. It is therefore a valuable tool for voice production to develop a musical ear and musical brain. Bhramari has an immediate relaxing effect on the brain. If it is practiced few minutes every day, it can trigger the creative and speech centres in the brain and enhance all types of memory. It stimulates the vocal cords, the larynx, cleans the resonators, makes flexible the articulators and increases the breath capacity. It develops the hearing, listening and perceiving capacity. Bhramari is part of the classical teaching of Indian music.

Speakers/singers are advised not to do Sheetali and Sitkari Pranayam-s, inspite of their benefits. Vocal activities and singing need a higher than normal temperature of the voice box and mouth, and these Pranayam-s cool down the mouth and voice box.

6. Omkar

Omkar is a combination of sounds of the alphabets A (as in along), U (as in put) and M (as in sum). It is pronounced in many different ways for achieving different results. It is pronounced basically as A+U+M as three sounds or as O+M (as in dome) as two sounds, with different variations.

Another name for Omkar is Udgitha. In Chhandogya Upanishad, the importance of Omkar for voice and singing are mentioned clearly. It says that Omkar, Prana and Swara (musical note) are same words for one concept. The word Udgitha derives from the Sanskrit root '*gai*' which means 'to sing', combined with the suffix '*uchha*' which means of high caliber. So Udgitha means 'song of high caliber'.

Yoga gives a lot of importance to Omkar – the Cosmic Sound. Patanjal Yogadarshan has suggested Omkar Japa Sadhana (recitation) for attaining Samadhi or Ultimate Salvation. The approach of Yoga being holistic, this can be applicable to every positive goal.

तज्जपस्तदर्थभावनम् || १.२८ ||

Omkar should be chanted and meditated upon. || 1.28 ||

ततः प्रत्यक्चेतनाधिगमोऽप्यन्तरायाभावश्च || १.२९ ||

Omkar Sadhana helps to attain the higher level of Consciousness and remove obstacles in the path of Yoga.
|| 1.29 ||

व्याधिस्त्यानसंशयप्रमादालस्याविरतिभ्रान्तिदर्शनालब्धभूमिकत्वानवस्थितत्वानि

चित्तविक्षेपास्तेऽन्तरायाः || १.३० ||

It removes 1) Vyadhi – diseases, 2) Styan – heaviness of the body, 3) Sanshaya– doubt, 4) Pramad – negligence
5) Alasya – lethargy, 6) Avirati – desire,
7) Bhranti Darshan – hallucinations,
8) Alabdha-bhumikatva – to think negatively that one can never gain from the sadhana and
9) Anavashitatvani – mental instability. These 9 are Chitta viksheph – mental distractions.
Omkar removes all these obstacles|| 1.30 ||

One should start Omkar Japa in the 'vaikhari vani' i.e. the mouth. Gradually, after some days or months, the japa moves to the depths to 'madhyama'. Here the chanting happens in the mind. When this is achieved the chanting moves further to a subtler level of 'pashyanti'. Here there is no action. It is a passive hearing of the inner sound of the chakra-s which sounds like 'Om'. Then gradually, over a period, the sadhaka, person who is practicing, moves to the 'para vani' where he experiences the anahat nada, the soundless sound, the Cosmic Sound, the unmanifested form of Omkar.

In Omkar Shatakam, Bhakta Vamana explains the manner in which Omkar should be pronounced or chanted. Bhakta Waman says:

संततं तैलधारैव दीर्घघण्टा निनादवत् |
दीर्घ प्रणवमुच्चार्य गंभीरम्शंखनादवत् ||

santatam tailadhaaraiva dIrghaghaNTaa ninaadavat ||
dIrgham praNavamuchchaarya
gambhIramshankhanaadavat||
meaning: Omkar should be pronounced with long consistency like a continous and uniform flow of oil, should sound like a continous ringing of a bell, and should sound deep and resonant like the sound of a counch.

When Omkar Sadhana is practiced with the help of a tuned

tanpura(Indian drone instrument) it helps a speaker/singer in many ways. It helps to strengthen the lung capacity. It improves the timbre i.e. the texture of the voice. It practically removes all the disorders of the voice. It makes the voice sweet and melodious. Apart from this, it strengthens the mind by removing its stresses.

Omkar Sadhana helps a yogi to remove the obstacles in his Sadhana. In a similar way, speaker/singers' obstacles, in the path of learning, teaching and performing are removed, gradually. Voice disorders (including hearing disorders) are also removed. The voice becomes light and healthy. The speaker/singer finds his own answers to his doubts very easily. His lethargy is removed and he always feels fresh to practice and perform. He gets disinterested in negative desires. His mind remains steady and does not switch to vices. He always thinks positively about his performances and goal. His mind is never imbalanced. He creates a very positive auric field around him. In general obstacles tend to keep away from him.

The vaikhari chanting of Omkar starts in the mouth with 'a', moves to 'oo' in the throat, moves to 'mm' in the chest and further becomes more nasal moving towards the naval and head together. It creates vibrations in all the Chakra-s. We should remember that the Charka-s, being located in the Pranic body, are not stationary. They keep on shifting about one to two inches from their sthana or base. A note chosen for the chanting will vibrate with maximum intensity in its sthana i.e. its base, with the particular frequency of the Chakra-s. The vibrations will then percolate to other Chakra-s and Sthana-s, like ripples of a pond. eg. The note C with plus or minus half note will vibrate the Mooladhar Chakra. If the C note is chanted with great intensity, its vibrations will surely reach the Ajna chakra too. It is the intensity of the note that decides how far the vibrations would reach.

When we chant Om in a specific note with a tuned tanpura,

the 'Om' resonates multifold. It vibrates not only the body, but the vibrations reach the inner depths and outer surroundings together. This helps to purify the surroundings, body, mind, emotions and intellect. Our speaking and musical ability, hearing capacity, sound and musical memory, voice quality, speaking and singing capacity and above all our creative capacity are amplified multifold by chanting or singing of Omkar.

Chanting of Omkar in vaikhari or madhyama makes the brain waves vibrate at alpha or the meditative level. This helps the 'Prajna' and 'Pratibha' i.e. the highest intellect and creativity, to be aroused. This can further activate the latent potentials. When the chanting reaches the depths of pashyanti and para, the brain waves reach the Gamma level, which is the higher meditative level.

A Speaker/Singer is blessed by this 'Prajna' and 'Pratibha', which helps him not only as good performer, but good person, as well. This helps him to find and go in search of the subtle form of sound that is the 'Anahat Nad', which is our inner voice.

7.Meditation and Nadadharana:

Meditation is of two types – active and passive. Both help in the process of stress releasing and lead us to the path of holistic health – health of all the five kosha-s. There are many schools and techniques of meditation. All are helpful. I have designed this technique of editation for ear training, musical training, understanding of shruti-s, understanding the concepts of sound, tress releasing and of course, healing.

Nadadharana is a type of meditation, done with the help of concentrating on the music of the tanpura. I have developed this technique of meditation as an integration of music learning and meditation techniques I have followed. The word and technique of Nadadharana, where 'nada' means sound and '*Dharana*' means concentration in Sanskrit , is new to the concept of Yoga as well as music. I have been using this meditation technique since long. A primary knowledge of music is not necessary for this meditation. It can be practiced by anyone.

Apart from general benefit of meditation, this meditation helps ear training. It can enhance the understanding of the concept of shruti-s, ragas (unique Indian Musical Scale). It helps in balancing the energy levels of all the kosha-s. It helps in emotional and mental balance, which further improves the quality of voice, as well as singing. This meditation can break open latent potentials, which lie in a seed form. It also increases the pranic energy level which enhances the qualities of voice, making it energetic and confident, with a rich texture.

8.Prayer:

Prayer is a remembrance and invocation of the Ishwara, the Supreme Cosmic Energy. (It can be called as per the choice of the Sadhaka, practitioner, according to his likings, cultural conditioning and beliefs. If the Sadhaka is an atheist, or very materialistic and non-believer of unseen world, he can just call it as Energy). Here the mind is prepared by accepting the Superiority of the Cosmic Energy. This makes it possible for flexibility required for the subtle changes during the Yoga Practice.

9.Sankalpa (Resolution):

Here we invoke the Supreme Cosmic Energy to work on us. This helps the energy receiving centres, the Chakra-s and Nadi-s to be cleansed, prepared and opened for receiving more energy. It helps channelizing of the energy received to the direction of our goal. This Resolution also helps to accelerate the growth and the healing process. It improves our understanding level. Here the Intellectual Kosha is given positive instructions as affirmations. These instructions then percolate the grosser kosha-s and affect the physical level.

Sankalpa and prayer should be practiced together, as they are complimentary to each other. Both these practices help us to link our conscious and subconscious levels. We have to remember that energy is available in abundance to any person, at any given time. But, as humans we create innumerable blocks which obstruct the energy flow. Prayer and Sankalpa together start the healing and cleansing process on a subtle level.

M. Comparison between Yoga Practice and Other Exercises for Speaker/Singers

As we study the details of speakers'/singers' physiology and the process of training the organs for better functioning and their enhancing, we will be able to understand the importance of Yoga to all speakers'/singers. For developing any of the Vocal activities, the higher brain functions need to be developed. This is where Yoga has an upper hand over other musical and general exercises. Let us compare. Yoga Practices and General and Musical Exercises for speaker/singers, and the factors that are influenced by them. See chart 3.7

Comparison between Yoga Practice and Other Exercises for Speakers/Singers

Factors Involved	General and Musical Exercises	Yoga Practice
Approach	Limited/Narrow	Holistic
Kosha-s Involved	Physical and sometimes Pranika	All five Kosha-s
Works on	Manifested potentials	Manifested as well as Latent Potentials
Value Education	Not developed or enhanced	Automatically inhibits better and better values in our life
Base	Performance based, learning and teaching is also performance based	Performance based, as well as holistic learning & teaching based cultures holistically
Development of Quotients	Does not work on improving such quotients	Intelligence Quotient(IQ), Emotional Quotient(EQ), Spiritual Quotient(SQ) and Musical Quotient(MQ) all are improved together
Pattern of Exercises	Active Pattern	Active and Passive Pattern
Basic Voice Quality	Remains as it is	Can be modified
Mental Peace	Temporary limited to the actual singing period	More of a Permanent nature lasts for a very long span of time
Energy Enhancement	Sometimes	Always
Age for Learning and Enhancing Skills	Does not give results after a certain age (since they work more on the physical body)	Can enhance qualities at any age (since it works on the Pranika, Mental, Intellectual and Bliss bodies together)
Qualities Involved	Peripheral	Peripheral and Inner
Cost of Learning and Practicing these Exercises	Quite costly	Quite cheap, many times does not require any cost
Development of Other Skills	No	Many other skills are automatically developed.
Stimulation to Chakra-s	Does not stimulate	Stimulates them
Balancing of the Left and Right Brain Functions	Usually remains imbalanced as this factor is generally ignored	Works for betterment of balancing. Special attention is giving to the balancing factor.

chart. 3.7

Swara/note		Frequency (equi-tempered Scale)	Associated Chakra		Location In Body	Sense	Bija Mantra
Indian	Western		Sanskrit	English			
White 1	C4	261.63 Hz.	Mooladhar	Root	Anus	Smell	Lam - लं
White 2	D4	293.66 Hz.	Swadhishthan	Hara/sacral	Intestine	Taste	Vam - वं
White 3	E4	293.66 Hz.	Manipur	Solar Plexus	Stomach	Sight	Ram - रं
White 4	F4	349.23 Hz.	Anahat	Heart	Heart	Touch	Yam - यं
White 5	G4	392.00 Hz.	Vishuddha	Throat	Throat	Hearing	Ham - हं
White 6	A4	440.00 Hz.	Ajna	Third Eye	Forehead	Esp (extra Sensory Perception)	Sham - षं
White 7	B4	493.88 Hz.	Bindu	-	Top Back Of The Head	-	-
White 8	C5	523.25 Hz.	Sahastrar	Crown	Cortex	Cosmic Awareness	Om - ॐ

Chart 3.8

113

Conclusion

The five elements and the Pranayam kosha are the switching stations of converting energy to matter, from quantum level to the material level. The pancha jnanendriya-s are the necessary inputs, reporting the material activities to the mind and intellect. As soon as the intellect and mind decide the action, they send impulses and the intended job work is carried out by the pancha karmendriya-s by switching energy to matter.

' Yoga' is one of the best tricks to convert energy to matter at our will. Usually, the body and mind take us to an unwanted, unfruitful, non-practical fantasy ride. But, Yoga teaches us to master our body and mind mechanism.

'Yoga' is a beautiful word, and a life style, a blessing to mankind given by our seers of ancient times.

Today, the global boundaries are coming closer. The whole of mankind needs to join hands, needs to coordinate. The west and the east, the sciences and the arts, the ancient and the recent should coordinate, to evolve in a better future world.

If we really understand the metaphysics and 'quantum' of music, we will be able to understand why 'Yoga' works on the voice in a faster, better and holistic way than the general, traditional and the modern techniques of 'Voice Culture'. Though modern and traditional music and speech techniques are quite fruitful, as their approach is not a holistic one (that which affect quantum level and all our Kosha-s), they have many limitations and work more in a temporary style on the voice than making a permanent culturing.

Our 'Voice' is the reflection of our inner self. It is the blue print of our subtle bodies. By changing our voice we can change our personality, apart from being able to speak/sing well. If for this voice-culturing, we join hands with 'Yoga', it will work wonders. A speaker/singer may be a professional, a performer, a musicologist, a voice trainer, a teacher or may be he speaks/sings just as a daily routine or hobby, yoga will help one and all in satisfying the speaker/singer as well as the listener. The environment will further be enriched by positive vibrational field.

Though effective speaking or singing is an art, it is very helpful for a speaker/singer to know the science behind it. It not only helps him to be a better speaker/singer, but also adds to his holistic views. Knowledge of the science of singing and of voice production and 'inner awareness' developed by Yoga, makes a speaker/singer ponder over his style of speech/singing. He starts understanding his difficulties and faults and works on improving them.

Daily practice of Yoga adds luster and glory to the speaker's/singer's voice, helps him in solving his problems and keeps him mentally balanced even in difficulties.

In a nutshell, I would say –

Voice is the doorway
Of the quantum world
Listening is the root
To have a singing hold.

Voice is the 'Yoga'
Of head and the heart,
And Yoga is the voice
Of the whole in a part

Train yourself with Yoga
Add lusture to your voice
Ahat and the Anahat
Together you will rejoice

ll Hari Om Tat Sat ll

Appendix IA
Frequently asked Questions:

Q. I am not a singer. Can Yoga help to develop my voice?
A. Yes. These Yoga techniques will help everyone to improve their voice.

Q. I have severe voice problem. I have taken long treatments from surgeons. Can this technique help me?
A. Yes. As Yoga works holistically any type of problem with any degree can be resolved, at least to a high degree.

Q. I want to become a singer, but I have voice problem since my birth Can Yoga help me?
A. Yes. Even the voice problems, one is born with, can be improved upon. Mostly, such voice problem need a holistic treatment like yoga.

Q. I have an inferiority complex because I can not understand music, and I am embarrassed when people point this out to me (and laugh). Can yoga help?
A. Yes. Yoga will help to train the ear in such a way that it will improve the musical understanding of sound. It will help anyone at any level of understanding to fathom the deeper musical levels.

Q. My voice gets exhausted by the end of the day. I need to use my voice for riyaj i.e practice and programmes at least for 8-10 hours daily. Also, I do not have good breathing capacity. Can Yoga be beneficial?
A. Yes. Yoga will help to strengthen the voice muscles and the breathing capacity. Over and above, it will also help to tone the voice and breathing muscles, keeping you fresh and healthy till the end of the day.

Q. I have stage and exam fear. My voice trembles and I tend to forget all what I have learnt. Will Yoga really help to solve these problems?
A. Of course. In Yoga we work holistically. It will help to face all fears and handle all stresses. In fact, Yoga will help to get rid of these fears and stresses.

Q. I want to learn voice modulations. Can they be learnt with Yoga?
A. Yoga does not directly teach voice modulations. Still, Yoga will help you to overcome this problem. Voice modulation basically needs very good ear training, and healthy and strong articulators. Both these problems can be improved by Yoga.

Q. I have been taking part in many singing competitions. Judges always remark that I should have more energy in my voice. Can this be improved?

A. Yes. As we work a lot on the pranic level, the energy levels both physical and mental are enhanced.

Q. I have stammering problem since my childhood. Will Yoga help?

A. This problem will surely be solved as far as you do not have a structural problem. But, it will take time. So you will need to continue this practice for longer periods.

Q. I have a very bad vocal range. Also, my voice quality changes when I sing higher or lower notes. I want this problem to be solved. Is it possible with Yoga?

A. Though we don't directly work on voice range and register shifting, Yoga will still help. Firstly, the vocal and breathing muscles will become stronger. Secondly, the root cause of this problem lies in our stressed and rigid mind. These problems are worked upon, which will help to improve the voice range.

Appendix IB
Some Case Studies

I would like to share some cases of voice improvement for your benefit and understanding.

1. One client found it difficult to do Bhramari Pranayam. She felt heaviness and pricking sensation in the head. She was advised to do low pitched Bhramari with slightly open mouth. Within a week's time her capacity increased and she could do proper Bhramari.
2. Another client was already under doctor's treatment for Parkinson's disease and Hypertension. She was taking heavy drugs. Initially she was not able to sit on the floor. So she was allowed to sit on chair. After a week she could sit on floor by resting herself with the wall. After one more week she was able to sit properly. During the practice she improved her speech, which was initially without energy. By the end of one month she gained enough confidence, which reflected in her speech.
3. Before joining the workshop, this client was a tone deaf person. He reported me of his improvement in understanding the difference in the notes, while hearing music on television. After a week, he could sing along with the television songs.
4. One person reported that the harshness of his voice had lessened, his ability had increased and that his control over speech, specially to be able to stop talking where not necessary, had increased.
5. An elderly client was a Parkinson's patient facing a lot of difficulty in speech and writing. Initially he was unable to write even his own form. The feedback form was completed by him. He gained confidence in speech, and found speaking less difficult. He was refreshed by the workshop. Initially he could not sit on the floor. But, by the third weekend, he started sitting on the floor on his own.
6. Another lady reported of being able to sing better. She had gained confidence to sing. She felt that this had happened because of Omkar chanting. My personal observation was that this had happened because of a combination of kapalbhati and Pranayama.
7. A voice artist was facing many difficulties of voice modulation, hoarseness in voice and bad breathing capacity. She improved on all these factors.
8. A heart patient had a by-pass surgery few months before. He was told to do very light Kapalbhati and even very light Bhastrika (which is usually forbidden to heart patients). Just after the workshop ended he had his ECG taken, and specially came to my house to thank me and say that his ECG was now normal. He gave this credit to Yoga and the way he was

treated.

9. Another lady gave the first listening test without any compliant. She complained about not being able to understand the second test taken a month later. When I actually saw her result sheets, I came to know that she is one of the persons who have really excelled in the listening tests. At the first test she had no complaint as she did not even notice that she does not know. But, by the end of the month she improved her listening capacity so much that inspite that she could answer far better than the initial tests, now she was able to understand that she cannot solve all the questions and due to this frustration was complaining about not understanding.

10. A homeopath had a complaint of breathlessness and a weak voice at the start. She improved on both the aspects. Also, she felt relaxed.

I received phone calls from these clients requesting me to conduct Yoga workshops. They were eager to join these workshops on regular basis. This was an enough proof that they had enjoyed and benefited out of the techniques.

One more point worth noting is that even after a long time after the treatment, more than half the clients are still in regular contact with me and report that they have continued the Yoga practice at home.

All these points are of satisfaction and points showing real success of the Yoga techniques. Apart from the objective and proved results, the clients happiness, their raised confidence level, better voice quality, improved hearing capacity, mind stability and improved creativity are not only pleasing but are overwhelming to me.

Appendix IC
Improvement Of Voice At A Glance

'Prevention is better than cure'. That is why maintaining the Voice is equally important as is culturing and curing of Voice. Following are some do's and don't which would help to keep the voice away from problems. It also includes non-yogic techniques.

Here are some tips to take care of your voice in our daily routine:
1. Do not shout.
2. Do not whisper.
3. Refrain from too hot or too cold food.
4. Never overeat.
5. Drink sips of water (room temperature) between 1-2 hrs.
6. Never talk to the last breath. i.e. never use the residual capacity of lungs.
7. Sit or stand in correct posture: Backbone, neck, shoulders, chin and chest should be checked.
8. Never neglect voice or ear disorders or discomforts. Treat them immediately. Remember a stitch in time saves nine.
9. Never overstrain the voice and ears.
10. Relax the voice muscles and brain (by using relaxing techniques) as many times as possible.
11. Avoid using earphones when not necessary.
12. Take long breaths every ½ hr.
13. Give rest to your voice & ear in the 'rest' period. i.e. Try to avoid talking & listening unnecessary talks.
14. Do not breathe through mouth.
15. Avoid smoking or tobacco intake in any form.
16. Release extra stress of hearing & talking by pronouncing 'a' (as in avoid) or 'h' (as in her) while exhaling long breaths.
17. Chant 'Om' in-between short breaks.

Some methods to develop or culture the voice:
A. General Exercises
1. Pronounce r r r r, b r r r, p h r r r r, b h r r r r (pronunciation of 'r' should be on the lips in phrrrr, bhrrrr.)
2. Pronounce all the Sanskrit syllables daily.
3. Puff the mouth with air
4. Roll the tongue
5. Nasal humming in different pitches is a good exercise.
6. Making Faces, mocking
7. Yawn with closed mouth helps articulation better.

B. Music Exercises – Indian Music Lessons

1. Listen to the tanpura for a while. Try to understand the differences in the Swar-s, their volume differences, the laya of the tanpura, etc.
2. Hum prolonged 'Sa', your key note, at least 3 times
3. Hum sa, pa, sa, etc. for a few minutes daily.(Hum musical fifths in your scale)
4. Allot separate time for riyaz/practice, of every section of the music. eg. mandra sadhana, tara sadhana, aalap, taan, voice stability, sur, tala, meend, gamak, khatka, vilambit, drut, etc.
5. Listen analytically to your own voice details

C. Yogic Practice

1. Omkar – A + U + M + nasal awareness
2. Trataka
3. Kapalbhati
4. Neti (once a week)
5. Kapalarandhra Dhauti
6. Breathing – Abdominal, Chest and Shoulder
7. Brahma Mudra
8. Sinha Mudra
9. Nada Dharana
10. Pranayam – Ujjayi, Bhastrika, Bhramari

Using the Microphone

Microphone is our extended voice. So, equal care should be taken in selecting and using it.

1. Holding style and distance should be adjusted properly.
2. Avoiding blasts in articulation has to be worked upon.
3. Use speakers' or singers' microphone as is necessary.

Appendix IIA
Glossary – Meaning of Sanskrit Words

Word/term/aphorism	Meaning	Page nos.
Adhah	Lowermost	82
Adi shankaracharya	Name of an Indian sage, philosopher	80
Adilla	Khahula Voice in middle octave	17
Ahankara	Ego	61,64
Ahat	Sound formed with friction	78-80, 115
Alabdha bhumikatva	To think negatively that you will never gain from the sadhana	107
Alasya	Lethargy	107
Amla	Sour	75,76
Anahat	Sound formed without any friction	80,107, 109,115
Anavashitatvani	Mental unstability	107
Apara	Devoid of vibrations	82
Asana-s	Physical postures	88,95
Asphuta	Softly spoken	17
Atman	The real self within; the soul	56,57
Avadhanavan	A voice neither too loud nor too soft	16
Avirati	Desires	107
Ayurveda	Ancient hindu medical system based on the vedas.	21,56,57,72, 74,75,83
Bandha	To bind, the binding of prana; a psycho-muscular energy lock	58,88-91,93, 102-105
Bandha-jalandhar	Chin lock	103
Bandha-jivha	Tongue lock	102
Bandha-moola	Contraction of the anal region	104
Bandha-udiyan	Diaphragm lock	103
Bhagwat geeta	A treatise of a dialogue between krishna and arjun on yoga by maharshi vyas	59
Bhakti (yoga)	Yoga of devotion	59
Bhranti darshan	Hallucinations	107
Bindu	The spark of energy which has the potential to create and transform	68,69,71,72, 81,82,113
Bindu visarga	The residing area of bindu in our body	68,71,82
Bombaka	Voice derived from vata	17,75

Brahma granthi	A knot in the anal region in the kundalini	85
Buddhi	Individual Intelligence	61,62,64
Chakra	Wheel, the energy plexus in the pranic body	67,68,72
Chakra-ajna	Third eye chakra	70
Chakra-anahat	Heart chakra	70
Chakra-bindu	Chakra lies between the anja and sahastrar chakra	71
Chakra-lalana	Chakra situated near the soft palate	71
Chakra-manah	Chakra situated lower forehead	71
Chakra-manipur	Solar plexus	69
Chakra-mooladhar	Root chakra	66
Chakra-s	Plural of chakra	21,68,69,80,83, 85,107,108,110,112
Chakra-sahastrar	Crown chakra	66,71
Chakra-soma	Chakra situated above ajna	71
Chakra-swadhishthan	Sacral	68
Chakra-talu	Lalana chakra	71
Chakra-vishuddha	Throat chakra	70
Chitta	The platform where manas, buddhi (a lesser form of mahat) and ahankara work together	58,64,71,81,107
Chitta vikshepaha	Mental distractions	107
Dharana	Concentration; the sixth limb of ashtanga yoga	58,88,89,104,109
Dhauti	Cleansing	92,93
Dhwani	Rich on account of harmonics	79
Dhyana	Meditation; the seventh limb of ashtanga yoga	58,59,88,89
Dhyana yoga	Yoga of meditation	58
Gambhira	Full and loud	17
Gatra veena	The body-lute	72
Ghana	Voice that is pleasing and steady	16,17
Guna-rajas	Motion, the quality of energy, life and activity	60,61
Guna-s [1]	Prime qualities of prakriti – sattwa, rajas, tamas	60,61,75
Guna-s [2]	Qualities of dosha-s – they are 25 in number	73
Guna-sattva	Balance, the quality of light, intelligence and illumination	60,61,73,75
Guna-tamas	Resistance, the quality of matter, passivity and a dwelling place of latent potentials	60
Hansa-upanishad	Name of an upanishad	82

Hasta	Hand	98
Ishwar	Cosmic lord	63,64,110
Japa	Chanting	106,107
Jeevatma	Individual soul	59,87
Jnana (yoga)	Yoga of wisdom/knowledge	59
Jnanendriya-s	Sense organs	61,62,63,114
Kaivalya	Synonym of samadhi	59
Karma yoga	Yoga of action	59,60
Karmendriya	Motor organ	61,62,63,114
Kashaya	Astringent	75
Kathora	Harsh	17
Kattu	Pungent	75
Khahula	Voice derived from kapha	17,75
Komala	Soft	17
Kosha	Body, sheath	21,64,88,89,104, 109,110,112,114
Kosha-anandamaya	The blissful body	64,65,88
Kosha-annamaya	The physical or food body	64,65,88
Kosha-manomaya	The mental body	64,65,88,104
Kosha-pranamaya	The pranic body, the auric body, the bio-electrical energy field	64,65,88,104
Kosha-vidnyanamaya	The intellectual body	64,65,88,110
Kriya (Yoga)[2]	A Yoga technique	58
Kriya – neti	Cleansing process – cleaning the nasal passage	93
Kriya (Shuddhi kriya)[1]	Cleansing process	88-93
Kriya-agnisar	Cleansing process – of flapping the abdominal muscles fast	91
Kriya-dhauti-danda dhauti	Cleansing of stomach with water using a rubber catheter	93
Kriya-dhauti-jaladhauti	Cleansing of stomach with water by vomiting it	92
Kriya-dhauti-vesan dhauti	Cleansing process – massaging the nasal passage with rubber catheter	92
Kriya-dhauti-jivhamooladhauti	Cleansing process – cleaning the root of the tongue	92
Kriya-dhauti-kapalarandhradhauti	Cleansing process – massaging the hard palate	92
Kriya-dhauti-karanarandhradhauti	Cleansing process – massaging the opening of the ear canal	92
Kriya-jalaneti	Cleansing process – cleaning the nostrils with water	93
Kriya-kapalbhati	Cleansing process – heavy exhalations	91

Kriya-sutraneti	Cleansing process – massaging the nasal passage with rubber catheter	94
Kriya-trataka	Cleansing process – gazing without blinking	90
Kundalini	The storehouse of energy (situated in the mooladhar chakra)	58,68,82,85
Lavan	Salty	75
Laya	Tempo,speed	8,20,74,93
Laya yoga	Yoga of dissolving	58,59
Leena	humble	17
Madhura [1]	A voice that is melodious and excellent even in high registers	16,17
Madhura [2]	Sweet taste	75,76
Mahabhoota-aapa	Water	62
Mahabhoota-agni	Fire	62
Mahabhoota-akash	Ether	62
Mahabhoota-prithvi	Earth	62
Mahabhoota-s	Elements	61,62,64
Mahabhoota-tej	Fire	62
Mahabhoota-vayu	Air	62
Maharshi	Spiritually highly advanced sage	58,64
Maharshi patanjali	Author of the text 'patanjal yoga sutras'	64
Mahat	Cosmic intelligence	61,64
Manas	Mind	61,64
Masa	Month	76
Mishraka	Voice derived from a combination of vata,pitta, kapha	17,75
Moksha	Liberation, self-realization	59
Mudra	A hand or body posture which works on the electro-magnetic body	58,88,89, 90,98,102
Mudra-ashwini	Body posture – contraction and expansion of anal muscles	100
Mudra-brahma	Body posture – a series of four positions of the neck	100
Mudra-jnana	Hand posture	101
Mudra-linga	Hand posture	101
Mudra-prana	Hand posture	101
Mudra-sinha	Lion posture	99
Mudra-yoga	Body posture – done in vajrasan or padmasan	98
Nada [1]	(Na pronounced as nu in Nut) Vibrate, pulsate, flow – sanskrit root of the word nada	78

Nada [2]	(Na pronounced as na in Nazi)	
	Anything that vibrates or	59,62,68,
	pulsates, here sound	72,78-80
Nada-bindu-upanishad	Name of an upanishad	81
Nadabrahma	The vibratory universe	78,81
Nadadharana	Meditation of Nada	109
Nadayoga	Yoga of sounds	59,80
Nadi-s	The energy channels	21,66-68,88,
	in te pranic body	91,92,110
Narata	Voice derived from pitta	17,75
Nihssara	Voice without emotions,	
	Indifferent Voice	17
Omkar	The cosmic sound	64,88,89,106-109
Padmasan	Lotus posture	96-98
Pancha	Five	61,62,74,114
Paramatma	Cosmic soul	59,87
Parvatasan	Mountain posture	97
Patanjal yogadarshan	A text on 'yoga' by	
	maharshi patanjali	58,106
Pawanmuktasan	Wind releasing posture	95
Prajna	Wisdom	109
Prakriti	Premordial nature	60,61,63,64,66,73
Prana	Life force energy	64-67,74,86,89,95,
		98,101-104,106
Pranayam	Breathing techniques	
	with awareness	102,104,105,
Pranayam-bhasrika	Breathing technique of	
	heavy inhalations and exhalation	105
Pranayam-bhramari	Breathing technique with humming	105
Pranayam-sheetali	Breathing technique for cooling effect	106
Pranayam-sitkari	A type of pranayam that is cooling	106
Pranayam-ujjayi	Breathing technique exhalations	
	with friction in the throat	105
Pranic	Of prana	65,66,68,72,84,
		90,104,108,110
Pratibha	Imaginitive power	109
Purusha	Pure consciousness	60,63,64
Rishi	Sage	58
Ritu	Season	76
Sadhaka	A person who practices yoga	107,110
Sadhana	Practice, rehearse	80,106-108
Sama veda	A veda – origin of indian music	1
Samadhi	A state beyond mind	58,59,106,

Samatvam yoga uchyate	Yoga means a perfect balance	60
Sangeet Ratnakar	A music treatise by Sharangadev	16,67,78,83,85
Sankalpa	Resolution	88,110,111
Sankhya	A style of .indian philosophy	60
Sanshaya pramad	Doubting	107
Saptaka	Scale; octave	67
Saptaka-madhya	Octave - middle	67
Saptaka-mandra	Octave - lower	67
Saptaka-tara	Octave – upper	67
Sarvangasan	shoulder stand	95
Sharangadev	Writer of the treatise 'Sangeet Ratnakar'	83
Shavasan	A relaxing posture	98
Shravaka	Loud voice, which can be heard at a long distance	16
Shruti	Microtone (there are 22 shruti-s in an octave)	6,66-68,72,79,80, 83,109,110
Snigdha	The voice which sounds sweet	16,17
Sphotavada	An indian science based on the silent explosion of 'the word'	83
Sthana	Home, residing place	66,67,108
Styan	Heaviness of the body	107
Tanmatra	Sensory potential or subtle element	61,62
Tanmatra-gandha	Smell	62
Tanmatra-rasa	Taste	62
Tanmatra-roopa	Sight	62
Tanmatra-shabda	Sound, word	62
Tanmatra-sparsha	Touch	62
Tanpura	A drone instrument used in Indian classical music	107-109
Tara	Sweetness in high octave	17
Tikta	Bitter	75
Trataka-antar	Gazing in the eyebrow centre with closed eyes with awareness	90
Trataka-bahir	Blinkless gazing at an object with awareness	90
Tristhanashobhi	A voice that is properly balanced in all the octaves and registers	16
Upanishad	Ancient Hindu philosophic treatise	58,62,81,82,85,106
Vani	Speech, manifested 'Nada'	79,80,85,107,109
Vani-madhyama	Speech - mental	79,80,85,107,109
Vani-para	Speech - transcendental	79,80,85,107
Vani-pashyanti	Speech - visual	79,80,85
Vani-vaikhari	Speech - coarse, physical	79,80,85,107,109
Vayuh	Prana, air element	74

Veda-s	Ancient hindu treatise	1,72
Vyadhi	Diseases	107
Yogah samaadhihi	'yoga' means to go beyond mind towards the ultimate truth i.e. To go in 'samadhi'	59
Yoga shvasan	Breathing with inner awareness	104
Yogah karmasu kaushalam	Doing a karma with awareness in the most skillful way	60
Yogasana-s	Physical yogic postures	89,90,94,95
yogashchitta--vrttinirodah	Conscious restraint of the vibrations of the chitta (subtlest part of the mind)	58
Yuja	Join	59

Appendix IIB
Glossary – Meaning of English Words

Word/term	Meaning	Page nos.
Acoustic	Audio	33
Anterior	Front	24,25
Articulators	The body organs which	2,12,22,23,27,29,
	help in modulation of voice	50,83,99,105,
Aspiration	Blasts in the voice like 'h'	27
Assimilation	Absorption	69,73
Breath control	The control of	
	breathing movements	9,40,70,77,86
Breathing capacity	It is the lung capacity,	3,6,7,9,38,39,74,
	vital capacity	77,91,95-97,101,105
Cognitive	Regarding perception	42
Consciousness	A wakeful state; awareness	41,44,59,60,65,
		66,71,78,80,81,87,106
Crooning	Singing, uttering	18
Drone	A continuous sounding of	
	notes in the background	107
Enunciation	Diction	58
Falsetto	A style of phonation or voice modulation	18
Intercostal muscles	The muscles that bind the ribs	8,28,50,96
Lesion	Cut, scratch	29
Lung pressure	The air pressure exerted by the lungs	2
Muscle Strength	Physical force that can be	
	exerted by muscles	77
Muscle tone	The sustaining power of muscles	8,77,94
Neoplastic	Pertaining to abnormal growth, tumor	29
Optimum	Best possible	8,12,20
Phonation	The sounding process	
	by the vocal cords	1,2,9,10,12,19,27,28,70
Posterior	Back, behind	24,25,29,43
Primordial	Primal, elemental	60
Resonance	The effect created by the sounding	
	of different harmonics and	
	overtones along with the	
	phonated/produced sound	2,19,30,31,74,103
Transcend	Go beyond	65
Tremolo	Special type of vibrations given	
	to the voice intentionally	18
Truncation	Cutting off, shortening	27

| Vibrato | Special type of vibrations given to the voice, intentionally | 18 |
| Wobbling | Unwanted shaking of the voice | 8,18 |

Appendix III
Bibliography

Books for Music
- **Bharatiya Sangeet Ka Itihas'** Volume I by Ram Avatar Veer. Published by Radha Publications, New Delhi 1996
- **Sangeet Parijat'** of Shri Ahobal Pandit, translation and commentary by Pt. Kalindaji. Published by Sangeet Karyalay Hatharas
- **Sangeet Ratnakar'** Volume I by Sharangadeo, commentary by Dr.G.H. Taralekar. Published by Maharashtra Rajya Sanskriti Mandal, Mumbai.
- **22 Shrutis** by Dr. Vidyadhar Oke published by Sanskar Prakashan, Mumbai
- **Sangeet Visharad** by Vasant, published by Sangeet Karyalaya, Hatharas
- **Shri Gandharva Ved,** by Pt. Vasant Madhav Khadilkar published by Shri Gandharvaved Prakashan, Pune
- **The Natyashastra** by Adya Rangacharya, published by Munshiram Manoharlal Publishers Pvt. Ltd., New Delhi
- **Natyashastram** by Shri Satyaprakash Sharma, published by Choukhambha Surbharati Prakashan, Varanasi.

Books for Yoga
- **A Systematic Course in the Scientific Techniques of Yoga and Kriya,** by Swami Satyananda Saraswati, Bihar School of Yoga, Munger, Bihar.
- **Anandyoga** By Shrikrishna Vyavahare, published by Ghantali Mitra Mandal, Thane.
- **Dhyan Prachiti** by Swami Anand Rishi, published by Navin Prakashan, Pune.
- **Hansopanishad**
- **Lectures on Yoga** by Swami Rama, published by The Himalayan International Institute Of Yoga Science and Philosophy, Pennsylvania
- **Nadabindu Upanishad**
- **Patanjal Yogadarshan Ek Abhyas** by Swami Anand Rishi, published by Rajahans Prakashan
- **Pranayam** by Sadashiv Nimbalkar, published by Yogavidyaniketan, Mumbai
- **Pranayam Darshan** by Yogacharya Shrikrishna Vyavahare, published by Ghantali Mitra Mandal, Thane
- **Raja Yoga** by Swami Vivekananda published by Advaita Ashram, Kolkata
- **Swasthya Evam Yoga Chikitsa** written and published by Dr. Dattatraya Vaze, Pune.
- Translation of **Hatha Yoga Pradipika** published by Kaivalyadham, Lonavala

- **Yoga And Ayurveda'** by David Frawley, published by Motilal Banarsidass Publishers, Delhi
- **Yoga for Health, Healing and Harmony** by Yogacharya Shrikrishna Vyavahare and Dr. Ulka Natu. Published by Ghantali Mitra mandal, Thane
- **Yoga Nidra** by Swami Satyananda Saraswati. Published by Yoga Publications Trust, Munger, Bihar.
- **Yoga Tarang** monthly magazine, of Ghantali Mitra Mandal, Thane

Books for Voice Culture, Physiology and Anatomy:
- **Anatomy and Physiology for Nurses** by Evelyn Pearce published by Faber and Faber Ltd., London
- **Anatomy and Physiology of Yogic Practices** by Dr. Makaranda Gore, published by Kancha Prakashan, Kaivalyadham, Lonavala
- **Atlas of Anotomy** by Trevor Weston, MD, MRCGP, published by Bookmark Ltd., Leicester.
- **Awaz Sadhana Shashtra** by Prof. B.R.Deodhar, Mumbai. Published by Mangal Prakasha, Nagpur, for Maharashtra Vidyapeeth Grantha Nirmiti Mandal.
- **Awaz Sureeli Kaise Karen** by Dr. Laxminarayan Garg published by Sangeet Karyalay, Hatharas
- **Bhashan Rang** by Ashok Ranade, published by Popular Prakashan, Mumbai
- **Journal of the Indian Musicological Society** by Dr. S.A.K.Durga
- **Text book of Science (Physiology) for I.C.S.E. Board exams.**
- **Voice Culture** by Dr.S.A.K. Durga published by Indian Musicological Society, Mumbai and Vadodara

Books for Psychology:
- **Psychology of Music** by Carl Seashore
- **Psychology of Musical Ability** by Shuter, Rasamund
- **Report of the Seminar on 'Psychology of Music'** of Jan.'75 published by Sangeet Natak Academy
- **Sangeetache Manas-shastra** by Dr. Premala Kale, published by Majestic Prakashan, Mumbai.
- **Sangeetache Manas-shastra** by Shyamala Banarse for Maharashtra Vidyapeeth Grantha Nirmiti Mandal, published by Shri Lekhan Vachan Bhandar, Pune.

Other books
- **Quantum Healing and Perfect Health** by Dr. Deepak Chopra
- **The Miracle of Music Therapy** by Rajendra Menon published by Pustak Mahal, New Delhi

Appendix IV
Shloka-s on Voice

Sangeet Ratnakar By Sharangadeva

Shloka-s On Types Of Voice

चतुर्मेदो भवेच्छब्दः खाहुलो नारटाभिधः ||
बोम्बको मिश्रकश्चेति तल्लक्षणमथोच्यते || ३.३९ ||

chaturbhedo bhavecchhabdah khaahulo naarTaabhidhah ।।
bombako mishrakashcheti tallakshaNamathochyate ।। 3.39 ।।

कफजः खाहुलः स्निग्धमधुरः सौकुमार्ययुक् ||
आडिल्ल एष एव स्यात् प्रौढश्चेन्मन्द्रमध्ययो || ३.४० ||

kaphajah khaahulah snigdhamadhurah soukumaaryayuk ।।
aaDilla eSha eva syat prouDhashchenmandramadhyayo ।। 3.40 ।।

त्रिस्थानघनगम्भीरलीनः पित्तोद्भवो ध्वनिः ||
नारटो बोम्बकस्तु स्यादन्तर्निःसारतायुतः || ३.४१ ||

tristhaanaghanagambhIralInah pittodbhavo dhvanih
naaraTo bombakastu syaadantarnihsaarataayutah ।। 3.41 ।।

परूषोच्चैस्तरः स्थूलो वातजः शांगीर्णोदितः ||
एतत्संमिश्रणादुक्तो मिश्रकः सान्निपातिकः || ३.४२ ||

paruShochchaistarah sthUlo vaatajah shaangIrNoditah
etatsammishraNaadukto mishrakah saannipaatikah ।। 3.42 ।।

Natyashashtra By Bharatamuni

Edited By Pt. Kedarnath, Published By Satyabhamabai Pandurang, Nirnaysagar Press, Mumbai.

Shloka-S On Merits Of Good Voice

हृदात्तं ह्यदूरातुऋह्ह श्रूयते यस्मात्तस्माच्छ्रावक उच्यते ||
श्रावकः सुस्वरो यस्मादच्छिद्रः स घनः स्मृतः || ३२ . ३३ . १२ ||

hRdaattam (duraattu?) shrUyate
yasmaattasmaacchhraavaka uchhyate 11
shraavakah susvaro yasmaadchchhidrah sa ghanah
smRtah 11 32.33.12 11

अरूक्षध्वनिसंयुक्तः स्निग्धस्तज्ज्ञैः प्रकीर्तितः ||
मानप्रल्हादनकरः स वै मधुर उच्यते || ३२ . ३३ . १३ ||

arukshadhvanisanyuktah snigdhastajjnaih prakIrtitah
11
maanapralhaadanakarah sa vai madhura uchyate 11
32.33.13 11

स्वरेऽधिके च हीने च ह्याविरक्तोऽविधानवान् ||
शिरःकण्ठेष्वभिहितं त्रिस्थानमधुरस्वरैः || ३२ . ३३ . १४ ||

svare-dhike cha hIne cha hyavirakto-vidhaanavaan 11
shirahkaNTheShvabhihitam
tristhaanamadhurasvaraih 11 32.33.14 11

त्रिस्थानशोभीत्येवं तु स हि तज्ज्ञैः प्रकीर्तितः ||
कपिलो व्यवस्थितश्चैव तथा संदष्ट एव च || ३२ . ३३ . १५ |
|

tristhaanashobhItyevam tu sa hi tajjnaih prakIrtitah l
l
kapilo vyavasthitaschaiva tathaa sandaShTa eva cha l
l 32.33.15 11

Profile
Saunvad – Centre for Music and Healing

Inroduction

Saunvad is, a Centre for Well-being
Let me explain, what these words mean

Saunvad in Sanskrit, has meanings a many
It means at its core, a Wonderful Harmony

Harmony between, the Part and the Whole
A perfect blend, of the Body and the Soul

Harmony between, Science and Art
Harmony between, the Head and the Heart

It is a Dialogue depicting, Beautiful and Right
A process which treads, from Dark to Light

Heal yourself with us, with love and pleasure
Saunvad Healing Centre - an experience you'll treasure

Our Mission

" …………..*Do not treat the disease, treat the patient*
………………..the part of the soul which is within the grasp of our senses is the body, and the part of the body which is beyond the grasp of the senses is the soul. The invisible body is the soul, the visible soul is the body. They are not two different things, they are not two separate entities, they are two different states of vibrations of the same entity…………….One day somebody asked Buddha, "Who are you? Are you a philosopher or thinker or a saint or a yogi?"Buddha replied, I am only a healer, a physician. Only a healer— I know something about the inner diseases and that is what I discuss with you."…………

Osho: From talk given to Medical Association in Ahmedabad, Gujarat.

A Healer is a helper, a catalyst in the process of gaining health. Illness is a sign that we lack harmony between the body and the soul. Illness may be physical, emotional, mental, intellectual, spiritual or a combination of these. There are blocks created in the channels of light and energy disconnecting their flow partially or fully. A Healer just helps to clear the blocks and reconnect the flow. The Healer helps the client understand that 'HE can Heal himself'. Dr. Newton Kondaveti has rightly said, 'we create our own reality'.

We would like to help you in this healing process by helping you to understand and experience the laws of nature in the process of evolution of the soul, and their application in our day to day life.

Residential and Non Residential Workshops on Yoga Therapy for Voice Improvement
(An exclusive feature of our workshop is - Healing Sessions with Past Life Regression Therapy)

Who can join
- Singers, musicians, people attached with a profession related to voice, like teachers, advocates, anchors, compeers, home makers, etc. from amateurs to experts
- Anybody interested in having a good and healthy speaking or singing voice
- Anyone interested in improving Voice Quality, Stamina, Breathing Capacity and Breath Control, Voice range, Voice Energy, etc
- Anyone interested in improving upon voice disorders, communication problems, stage fear, performance hazards, expressional abilities, language barriers, memory, etc
- Developing a better musical ear and hearing capacity
- Anyone with THYROID or ASTHMA problems.

Main Benefits
- Helps improve upon all the above points and general health
- Improves upon vocal disorders – both physical and mental - from a hoarse or squeaky voice to problems like stammering, stuttering, heavy and inflexible tongue, etc
- Improves articulation and Voice Modulation
- Makes voice stronger, more attractive and sweeter
- Increases breathing capacity and control over the breath.
- Increases hearing capacity, develops musical ear, improves audio memory
- Increases Voice Pitch Range, Voice Volume Range, Voice Energy, Voice Stamina
- Improves Expression and Creativity

Other Benefits
- Helps in correcting digestive disorders.
- Helps in correcting problems like high/low blood pressure, sleeplessness, fatigue, stress, etc.
- Helps in balancing the three dosha-s explained by Ayurveda

Non- Residential Workshops includes: An introduction to the topics under theory and practical mentioned for Residential Workshops.

Residential Workshop includes:
Theory:
• Understanding Basic Concepts of Voice – Modern and Metaphysical
• Taking care of the Voice – Diet, Vocal Habits, Registers, Pitch, Volume, home remedies, etc.
• Controlling Voice Problems
• Using the Microphone
• Managing and Understanding Articulation, Voice Modulation, Speaking v/s Singing, etc.
• Differences in Yoga techniques and other Exercises.
• Techniques of practicing lessons of Singing and/or Speaking.

Practical:
• General Breathing techniques
• Energy Building Yoga techniques
• Shuddhi kriya-s (cleansing techniques)
• Omkar, ,Yogasanas, Yoga Mudra-s, Bandha-s, Pranayam
• Meditation-s - active and passive types including Dynamic, Nadabrahma, Natraj, Nadadharana, Anapanasati, Gibberish, Yoganidra, etc.
• Mantra Sadhana
• Speech Exercises

Interactive:
• Lecture-demonstrations on healing through Ayurveda, Accupressure and Accupuncture, Reiki, etc
• Voice/yogic games, entertainment, etc.

Personal Tests (Pre/Post Parameters) and Guidance (both optional):
• Voice Tests
• Breathing Tests
• Listening /Hearing Tests
• Personal Consultaion and Guidance

Certificate Course in Yoga for Voice Culture (Available as Distant Learning)
Objective – Self-improvement of voice and managing the defects with Yoga. Getting trained to train and counsel others for the same

Course Syllabus in brief
1. Voice and speech – its importance and understanding.
2. Anatomy and physiology of Voice, taking care of voice.

3. Understanding related concepts from Indian Texts - Natyashashtra and Sangeet Ratnakar.
4. Yoga techniques – Shuddhikriya-s, asana-s, breathing techniques, pranayam, mudra-s, bandha-s, sankalpa, omkar, etc.
5. Yoga, nada – their understanding and classifications of nada and voice.
6. Concepts of Ayurveda, Diet.

Note:
Video and Audio cds of the course are available.

We also conduct Past Life Regression Healing Workshops and Therapist Training Workshops.

These workshops help one to experience and understand the higher dimensions and purpose of life helping us to live at our best . It also helps one find joy, peace, love, confidence, courage and the spark in life!

It can resolve issues related to:

Health: includes
- Physical issues - simple to complex, acute to chronic, unexplainable, undiagnosed, unresolved by other therapies, etc.
- Emotional issues –unwanted individual character issues like anger, lethargy, anxiety, greed, jealousy, etc.
- Mental issues – including stress, vices, recurring negative patterns, lack of clarity of thoughts, lack of confidence, over confidence, etc.
- Intellectual issues - growth and obstacles
- Spiritual issues – stagnation or obstacles in spiritual growth

Wealth: includes any financial issues

Relationship issues

Fears, Phobias, Addictions, etc.

Understanding the lessons to be learnt in this present life

This is done by accessing memories of the past, which are stored in the sub-consciousness mind. These memories are the root cause of the relevant issues.

The root cause could be in the past memories of this present life time or any one or more previous life times. The root cause could be either in the past memories of this present life time or any one or more of previous life times.

It helps one to retrieve energies from the past, transform the negative energy patterns into positive energy patterns and assimilate them into the present life situations.

Products

Music and Healing:

* Sangeet Haripath (Sant Jnaneshwar) set of 2 audio cd's of Marathi Devotional Songs, by Dr. Manjiree Gokhale
* Audio and Video CD's of Yoga for VoiceCulture
* Audio CD Nadadharana – including guided Nadadharana Meditation Meditation and Guided Yoganidra (Yogic Relaxation Technique
* Audio CDs Heal Yourself – Guided Rebirthing Breathwork and Past Life Regression

Books : By Swami Anand Rishi (Marathi)
* Punarjanmache goodh – A book on Reincarnation
* Patanjalyogadarshan - ek abhyas – A book on Patanjal Yogasutra-s
* Malaa umajlele osho – A book about Osho
* Hazar muddyansathi shambhar katha – anuvaad Translation of Osho's book
* Dhyan Prachiti – A book on different meditation techniques

Book : By Dr. Manjiree Gokhale

Manjulai (kavita sangraha) – My poetry book

Services
* Devotional Music Progarammes (Marathi and Multilingual) of Saints across Maharashtra, India and few other nations
* Career Guidance
* Audio Recording/Editing
* Music Direction
* Dance Choreography
* Dance Workshops: Special batches for Ladies

Library
A free reference library of books, audio cassettes, CDs and videos related to subjects like Music, Healing, Yoga, Philosophy and other related subjects.

www.ingramcontent.com/pod-product-compliance
Lightning Source LLC
Chambersburg PA
CBHW060505030426
42337CB00015B/1752